OUR BODIES
as the
GARDEN
of EDEN

NICHOLAS BRANCH

CONTENTS

Prologue

HOW IS YOUR GARDEN?

God trusts you

This book is grounded in the love and trust of the Creator of all things—who is infinite, unconditional love and light.

He trusts you.

God has always been my Father, my brother, my friend, my Savior—the one who spoke purpose into me when I was drowning in a river with no hope.

And now, I invite you into your own beautifully unique relationship with the Origin of all love and creation.

This is not just another book. Not another man. Not another voice telling you what to do or what to believe.

Because God believes in your ability to hear, feel, and experience Him— for yourself, in all His forms.

And so do I.

Let this be the beginning of a loving, ongoing conversation between you and the One who formed you.

If you're open to trusting that you *can* experience God directly, miraculous abundance is waiting.

Heaven on earth. Eden within you.

We are all invited to commune with a loving Father to receive more than we can imagine.

Let's take Him up on that offer, right here, right now—in our beautifully crafted bodies, our loving hearts, and our peaceful minds.

As friends, let's open our eyes to see our bodies not just as temples where God dwells, but as the Garden of Eden itself—the very garden the temple was created to reflect.

How is your garden?

Our first question—before routines, plans, or diagnoses.

Are you thriving?
Are you abundantly well?
Are you overflowing in peace?

Not "How much are you doing?"
Not "What do others think of you?"
Not "Are you succeeding?"

This book was born from the deep belief that true wellness begins with remembering who we are—beloved, whole, made in the image of God.

It is the synergy of faith and wellness, rooted in the truth that all good things come from a loving Father who calls you "very good."

Maybe right now everything feels like it's flowing.

Or maybe you're where I once was—lying on the floor, business collapsed, heartbroken, future uncertain.

Or again, lying in silence in the wake of divorce, away from my children, believing I was living my worst nightmare.

Even deeper in memory, I remember drowning in a river—body and spirit—crying out to God to erase me.

I didn't feel very good. I didn't feel worthy. I didn't feel like I was even worth existing in heaven or on earth.

And yet, I came back.

Not just to life, but to **Truth**:

That I am loved.
That I carry Eden within me.
That I am a child of God.

From The River to the Garden

The River told the story of what happened when I died and returned.

This book, *Our Bodies as the Garden of Eden*, tells the story of what happened when I chose to live—fully, intentionally, lovingly, and abundantly, just as God designed us to live.

It's about what it means to walk out our healing.
Not just the miraculous moments—but the daily miracles.
Not just the mountaintop highs—but holding our energy and space in any circumstance.

This book isn't a wellness plan.
It's an **invitation**—
To tend your own garden.
To partner with God.
To rediscover the divine harmony you were always meant to walk in.

In the Beginning

You may have heard the story before.
In the beginning: God, humanity, the garden.
Harmony. Wholeness. Connection.

And then—a piece of fruit.

Yes, a piece of fruit, distorted by deception and eaten in distrust.

Not because it looked evil—but because it looked good.

How often does the enemy twist the appearance of something—not for our good, to look pleasing to our eyes?

In the creation story, the garden was lost when we stopped trusting God's definition of "good."

Today, **wellness** is often lost in the same way.

We've been told so many things:

- *This* diet will save you.
- *This* pill is the answer.
- *This* trend is the truth.

Yet, here stands the voice of God, gently asking:
Will you trust Me with your wellness?

"Who But God is Good?"

In the Garden, one piece of fruit—something that seemed good—was called "not good."

Not because fruit itself was bad, but because eating it meant stepping outside of trust in God's voice.

The Garden story was never really about apples or diet—it was always about trust.

God wasn't keeping something from us.
He was keeping something for us.

A way of living rooted in His voice.
A rhythm of health that flows from trust.

This same theme echoes in Acts 10, when Peter heard a voice telling him to eat what had once been forbidden. Shocked, he resisted, but the Lord replied: *"Do not call anything impure that God has made clean."* (Acts 10:15).

The message was clear then, just as it was in Eden: God's voice is the ultimate guide.

His word, His timing, His love always carry life.

Can we trust Him?
Even when it doesn't make sense?
Even when the world screams otherwise?
Even when the rules we've clung to feel safer than His whisper?

This is where *The River* meets *Our Garden*.

From the moment God returned me to life, He began guiding me into wellness through trust:

Trusting His voice.

Trusting my body.

Trusting the people God placed in my life, each carrying gifts meant for one another—woven into our journeys so intricately that only in His divine tapestry could something so beautiful unfold.

Reunion of all Good Things

This book is not a rejection of science or modern health tools.
It is a **reunion**.
A sacred returning.

Where medicine and meditation, nutrition and prayer, therapy and scripture are no longer separated, but united—under the loving care of a Father who delights in our healing.

Religion and science were never meant to be at war.
They are both languages of a Creator who loves to speak to us.

This isn't about methods.
It's about **relationship**.
Listening for God's voice in all things.
And learning to walk with Him again—

In joy.
In trust.
In love.

Do you see your body as holy ground?
Do you see your nervous system as the wind through which God flows within your body?
Do you see your breath as sacred air from Heaven?

Do you see your bones as trees planted by water?
Your muscles as mountains carved by His hands?

You were not meant to survive.
You were created to **flourish**.

Our Body, The Temple

After Jesus's death and resurrection, the Temple was no longer a physical place.

It became people.
It became God's dwelling place in His children.
It became us.

The Temple was always meant to reflect something even older—
Even more foundational.

The Garden.

God walked with humanity there.
Before religion.
Before rules.
Before shame.

In Eden, everything was connected.
In your body—it still can be.

You are the new garden.
In you, Heaven longs to take root.

Come with me.
Let's tend this space together.
Let's see what grows.
Let's walk again in the cool of the day with our Father.

Let's return—
To love.
To wholeness.
To the Eden within.

Introduction

DO YOU SEE YOURSELF AS A PRECIOUS CHILD OF GOD?

W e begin with identity.
We begin with belovedness.

Not with striving.
Not with fixing.

That truth might feel foreign, uncomfortable, even impossible, depending on the voices that have shaped your life. But let me gently offer this:

Before you try to get better—before you chase a plan or a prayer—can you pause and consider:
What if your starting point isn't your brokenness, but your belovedness?

You are already precious.
Already chosen.
Already loved.

Self-Love

God has revealed clear wisdom to me about my priorities on this earth. It begins with myself and my wife—our oneness, and also our beautiful uniqueness. Loving one another as well as ourselves. Honoring the sacred union we've been given.

From that center flows our next priority: our children. Grounded in God's love, who is in all things.

It took me years to understand that placing myself first—in alignment with God—isn't selfish. It's stewardship.

- The world says hustle. And I hustled nearly out of connection with my family—the most precious gifts I never imagined I'd receive after drowning in that river.
- Religion says sacrifice. I've lost count of how many times the Lord had to pull me off a cross He already bore.

God's kingdom whispers something deeper:

"Love the Lord your God with all your heart, soul, mind, and strength... and love your neighbor **as yourself.**"

That "as" holds weight.

You cannot love others from an empty well.
Your love for others flows from the way you love yourself.
Self-love—rooted in divine love—becomes the wellspring of truly infinite unconditional love.

Who Are You in the Garden?

How do you view yourself?

Do you see yourself as a precious child of God?

Do you see someone bold, beautiful, creative, and grounded?
Do you see someone worthy of love, of pleasure, of purpose?

Do you see the man who can be courageous and vulnerable, open and strong?
Do you see the woman who is radiant, wise, powerful, and held?
Do you see someone God not only loves—but **delights in**?

Or has that view become clouded—by shame, by trauma, by religion, by pressure, by performance?

Take a breath.
Slow your body.
Notice what stirs inside you.

Can you hear the whisper of love underneath the noise, the negative self-talk, the enemy's voice.

It may not sound like much at first. Maybe it's a sigh. A sensation. A moment of softening.

The voice of God often comes quietly.

Sometimes like a warm hug in a tear-streaked bathroom.
Sometimes in the silence between children screaming, trying to do your best as a parent.
Sometimes in the tension of just making it through the day.

He's always known how to find you.
Even if you've been told otherwise.
Even if you've been told He's too holy for you.
Even if you've been told you don't belong.

He sees you.
Right now.
Not the cleaned-up version. Not the future you.
Just you.

He calls you *beloved*.

How Do You See God?

How you see God changes everything.

When I wrote *The River*, I shared what happened when I died and encountered the Lord.

Not as a distant monarch.
Not as an angry king.
But as the most loving presence I had/will ever experience.

Not judgmental.
Not punishing.
Just overwhelmingly, breathtakingly loving.

If you've only ever seen God through filters of fear and control, that can be hard to believe.

If your idea of God is someone who demands worship, throws lightning bolts, or keeps score—how could you possibly relax into love?

I've been there.

Even with the miracle of my own death experience, I still had to unlearn the false gods both the world and religion taught me to fear.

So let me say this clearly:
The God who knows you and made you in love—
Is not afraid of your questions.

He's not the insecure "gods" that humanity historical turned to in one way or the other (think the Greek or Norse gods).

He's not threatened by your doubts.
He isn't angry at your boundaries.
He doesn't need your performance.

He wants your **heart**.
Even the skeptical parts.
Even the tired parts.
Even the guarded parts.

Like the father in the story of the prodigal son, He runs to you.

If, like the older brother in the story, you try to earn His love, He gently invites you back into the truth of His unconditional embrace.

There is no perceived disconnection too wide for His grace.
The illusion of separation ends the moment we remember:
He never left.

Openness Is the Starting Gate

We don't begin with certainty.
We begin with **openness**.

When Jesus encountered the man lying beside the pool, He asked:

"Do you want to be well?"

That's still the question.

Do you want to be **right**?
Or do you want to be **well**?

The need to be right will close you.
It will defend your limitations.
It will argue with healing.
It will cling to identity in pain rather than transformation.

But openness...
Openness is a posture of grace.
It allows room for surprise. For softness. For renewal.

God doesn't need you to have everything figured out.
He's not looking for you to pass a test.
He's not asking for your resume.

He simply comes.
With no demands.
Only love.

Like a gentle rain on dry soil.
Like living water finding cracks in stone.

So here we are.

Welcome to this next part of the journey.

If *The River* invited you to see the miracle of your life,
Our Bodies as the Garden of Eden invites you to **live it**.

To tend your body with love.
To honor its systems and holy rhythms.
To listen to what your cells already know:

You are whole.
You are vibrant.
You are home.

Let's begin.

A Word about Journaling as Conversation with God

Throughout this book, you'll find invitations to pause.

Fully Present with God.

These are more than questions. They are doorways.

Each reflection moment is a space for you to step away from the noise, breathe deeply, and listen. Not just to your thoughts—but to God's voice within you.

This is not homework. It's holy dialogue. These are not journal prompts. They're invitations to sit with the Gardener Himself—to ask, to respond, to be still, to write what stirs.

Whether you answer with words, tears, images, or silence, these sacred pauses are designed to reconnect your spirit and body to God's presence.

Let this be your rhythm: read, breathe, ask, listen, and write. Let your pen become a vine. Let your words take root. Let God meet you there.

Part I

OUR GARDENS

Chapter 1

WHO'S IN YOUR GARDEN

The Garden of Eden wasn't just a paradise of beauty—it was a mirror of divine intimacy. It was the sacred space where humanity lived in total connection: to God, to self, to nature, to rhythm. There was no need to strive, to fix, to perform. Everything was whole, and everything was in relationship.

As we reflect on our own inner garden—our bodies, our souls, our breath—we begin to see echoes of Eden in our daily lives. The aches. The longings. The joy and the stillness. But who or what is living in our garden now? And how do we tend to it with love, wisdom, and awareness?

This chapter is an invitation—not a lecture. I don't come with all the answers, only the open hands of someone still learning. Together, let's walk through the gates of the garden within and ask:

Who's here with me now?

God: The Presence That Walks With Us

Let's begin with the One who walked in the garden in the cool of the day: God.

How do you see Him?

For many years, I wrestled with that question—shaped by how religion and the world often portray God. Is He a distant judge or a loving

Father? A tyrant king or a gentle friend? And if God is so powerful, why does evil so often seem louder, stronger?

I used to imagine strength as dominance.

The action hero archetype I grew up with shaped my view. But God's strength doesn't need to shout. His love *is* His power—and it's so powerful, grounded, steady, it doesn't have to prove anything.

In *The River*, when I encountered God after drowning, I didn't meet the world's version of power. I met love—a love that vanquishes evil and creates all that is good. I met peace. A peace that transcends all understanding. I met gentleness that felt like the deepest homecoming.

That version of God—the real one—is the truth I needed to return to in order to begin walking in the abundant life the Father has always offered us.

God still walks in gardens. Especially yours.

Fully Present with God

How do you view God in this season of your life? Is it different from the past? What shaped that view?

Take a moment to reflect on the picture of God you hold today. Is He near or distant? Gentle or demanding? How has your story, family, or church experience shaped this view? Write honestly—and invite Him to show you His true face of love.

_____

_____

_____

_____

_____

_____

_____

_____

_____

_____

_____

_____

_____

_____

_____

_____

_____

_____

_____

_____

Humanity: Made in the Image, Still in Process

After Adam and Eve hid, God called out, "Where are you?"

Not because He didn't know—but because He wanted them to *see* themselves. To pause. To notice.

So I ask you: **Where are you?**

Right now.

Not someday when you've figured things out.
Not when you've hit your goals.
Not when the pain is gone.

Right here. In your breath. In your body.

Do you see yourself as a beloved creation, made in the image of God? Or has that image been buried beneath shame, pressure, performance?

There were seasons when I only saw myself as a failure—someone who had to keep proving I was enough. I talked to my body like it was a slave, pushing it past exhaustion, never listening to its needs.

God sees us with eyes of love, even when we can't see ourselves.
He calls us out of hiding.
He says: **I see you. I made you. I still choose you.**

Fully Present with God

Where are you today? Who do you see when you close your eyes and picture yourself? How does God see you?

Close your eyes. Picture yourself as you are right now—tired, hopeful, messy, radiant. Then imagine God looking at you in that same moment. What's on His face? What words does He speak?

The Land: Stewarding Sacred Soil

In Eden, the land was alive—and humanity was called to tend it.

What if our bodies are that land now?

Our organs, bones, joints, and skin are not distractions from our spiritual life. They are the terrain of it. God formed Adam from the earth itself. We are made of matter, and *that matter matters*.

I used to think "my flesh" was the enemy. That holiness meant disconnection from my body. But what if holiness means alignment? Integration? Honoring the temple God formed with His own hands?

We can't love what we shame. We can't steward what we resent.

So how are you tending to your land?

Are you pushing through pain? Ignoring the signals? Judging your form instead of blessing it?

Our bodies are not mistakes to fix. They are gardens to tend.
And like all gardens, they speak.
Are we listening?

Fully Present with God

If your body had a voice, what would it say today? What does it need more of—or less of?

Listen gently. Your body might whisper, *I need more rest, I need water, I need joy,* or *please stop pushing me.* Write down what it's asking for, without judgment.

_____

_____

_____

_____

_____

_____

_____

_____

_____

_____

_____

_____

_____

_____

_____

_____

_____

_____

_____

_____

_____

Water: The Flow of Life Within

In Eden, rivers flowed freely, watering every living thing. Our bodies, too, are mostly water—fluid in constant motion, flowing life from cell to cell: blood, lymph, tears, sweat. Life moves through us.

What happens when that flow is blocked?

There have been seasons when I felt dried out—spiritually and physically. Dehydrated not just in my skin, but in my soul. Our bodies often reflect internal stagnation: fatigue, tension, inflammation.

Water invites us to soften. To surrender. To move with grace, not force.

Yes, are you drinking enough water—but also:
Are you giving your body permission to be in flow?
Are you releasing what no longer serves you?
Or are you holding tension like a clenched fist?

God's presence is like living water.
Not dammed-up doctrine. Not dry performance.
A gentle, continuous nourishing flow that brings healing.

Sky: The Breath of Eden

Scripture says God breathed life into Adam's nostrils—and humanity came alive.

Breath is sacred. It connects body and spirit. It is the invisible thread tying heaven to earth, keeping us here, keeping us now.

And yet, we forget to breathe.

Sometimes I catch myself shallow breathing—like I'm braced against life, just trying to survive. It takes me back to when I was a child, gasping for air as I nearly drowned in the river. My chest tight. My body panicked. Every inhale uncertain, every second desperate for the next. Survival breathing. Shallow, incomplete, afraid.

But I am not drowning anymore.
I am alive.
I am here.

Now, when I pause and receive a full breath, it feels like redemption. Like I am inhaling proof that God has carried me from fear into freedom. Each breath is no longer a gasp—it is a gift.

So I ask myself: *What am I afraid to fully receive?*

Because the way I breathe often mirrors the way I live. Half-in, half-out. Rushing. Bracing. Forgetting abundance.

Breath invites us back.
Breath invites us to pause.
Breath invites us to remember: we are alive.

So take one now.
Not just a sip, but a full inhale.
Slowly. Abundantly.

Let it fill your lungs without force, like light spilling into an open room. Let it remind you: You are already filled. Already sustained. Already beloved.

Each breath is God's kindness moving through your body. Each exhale is release. Each inhale, resurrection.

Fully Present with God

What is your breath like today? Quick? Heavy? Spacious? What might it be trying to say?

Place your hand on your chest or belly and notice your breath. Is it shallow, racing? Slow, deep, grounding? Let your breath be a teacher—revealing the pace of your soul

_____

_____

_____

_____

_____

_____

_____

_____

_____

_____

_____

_____

_____

_____

_____

_____

_____

_____

_____

_____

Trees, Plants, Animals: The Body's Living Ecosystem

Your body is alive with wisdom.

Each organ, each system, each signal is part of the garden God created: your skin, your digestion, your nervous system. You are not a machine. You are a living landscape.

We were never meant to dominate our bodies like tyrants. We were meant to tend to them like gardeners.

For years, I pushed myself—exercising through pain, suppressing symptoms, ignoring my body's requests. It wasn't servant leadership; it was a dictatorship.

The Father gently opened my eyes to the truth:
I was harming what I was meant to cherish.

Now I ask: *What does this part of my body need today?* Nourishment? Movement? Stillness?

When we listen, our bodies speak.

The Enemy in the Garden

It's a hard question, but we must ask: **Is there something in your garden that doesn't belong?**

Scripture tells us the enemy entered Eden not with fire, but with deception.

That's often how shame enters our own gardens—quietly, deceptively, planting lies about our worth, our bodies, our belonging in God's love.

Sometimes what doesn't belong is physical—pain, illness, dis-ease.

Other times it's mental or spiritual—old narratives, anxiety, fear, bitterness.

Even the enemy's presence didn't make Eden any less divine. It just revealed where truth was needed.

So don't wait for everything to be perfect to call it holy. **Holiness is not perfection. Holiness is wholeness.** It's honesty. It's presence.

God hasn't abandoned your garden.

He walks in it still and together you can release anything that doesn't belong there.

The Voice: Who Are You Listening To?

In Eden, multiple voices spoke: God's. The enemy's. Humanity's own.

Which voice is loudest in your life?

I've heard them all— the whisper of grace. The quiet affirmation: *You are loved, right now, just as you are.*

The voice of accusation, shame, and pressure to perform—what the wellness world often calls negative self-talk.

Sometimes, the voice I hear most is my own—trying to analyze, fix, figure it out.

God continues to invite me into something softer. Into a voice I don't have to earn or generate.

He is gently asking: *Will you let My voice lead again?*

How Do You Experience God?

If God is your loving Father, then boundaries become clarity.

If God is someone you can't trust, then boundaries feel like punishment.

You begin to create freely within the safety of grace—not to earn His love, but because you already have it.

That's where **true freedom is born.**

Not in restriction, but in rootedness.

What is your experience of yourself?

Pause and ask it again:

Do I believe I am a precious child of God?

If the answer is no—be honest.

Why not?
Who told you otherwise?
What story are you still carrying that makes you feel unworthy?

You are not alone in those questions. I've lived inside them. I've fought them in silence.

He sings over me a blessing—reminding me who I am in His eyes. Again and again, He speaks the truth of my identity.

Sometimes, it's the only thing I can hear and receive. Other times, I couldn't.

Still, God met me there.

He also speaks through others—a friend, a stranger, a child, a sentence you didn't expect to hear.

Not every word is from God, whether it rises from within you or comes from someone else.

When it is, I trust you'll feel it.

You'll feel the resonance.
You'll feel the love.

Because you are grounded in the One who is love and light—and anything that is not love's kind doesn't get to enter.

Your Body's Voice

Your body isn't your enemy.
It's a truth-teller—one that leans into the wisdom of the Father.

It warns before it breaks. It signals before it shuts down. I've learned that symptoms are sacred messengers—not inconveniences to ignore or override.

A tight muscle. A racing heart. A restless night.

What if these aren't failures, but invitations?

What if your body is asking: *Can you listen to me, even here? Can you love me better today?*

Discerning the Voice

Ultimately, that's what this chapter is about:
Discerning the voice of love from every other voice.

Letting love lead.
Letting fear fall away.
Taking what's true. Letting go of what's not.

Trusting your body, your soul, and your garden to know the difference.

Because when the fruit is real, you won't have to force it.

You'll taste it.

And it will be good. Because it comes from the Creator of all that is good.

Fully Present with God

What signs has your body been sending to you lately? Are you open to listening?

Think of the little signals—tight shoulders, restless sleep, bursts of energy, sudden tears. Your body is speaking. Are you willing to pause long enough to hear?

_____

_____

_____

_____

_____

_____

_____

_____

_____

_____

_____

_____

_____

_____

_____

_____

_____

_____

_____

_____

Priorities: What Matters Most in Your Garden?

If your life ended today, what would matter most?

What would you wish you had tended to with more care? Your relationships? Your rest? Your presence?

We often live like we have limitless time, scattering our energy everywhere, trying to please everyone.

God's invitation isn't to save the world on your own.

It's to walk with Him.

To trust Him with what you're holding.
To let Him carry what you were never meant to bear.

His yoke is light. His rhythm is grace.

What are you tending to today? And what needs to be gently pruned from your schedule so you can be more fully present?

Let this be your reminder:

You are loved. Your garden is sacred. And you are not alone in tending it.

Fully Present with God

What truly matters to you? What would you regret not tending to?

List the people, passions, and purposes that matter most. If today were your last day, what would you wish you had watered more faithfully?

_____

_____

_____

_____

_____

_____

_____

_____

_____

_____

_____

_____

_____

_____

_____

_____

_____

_____

_____

_____

_____

_____

Your Garden's Seasons

Every garden has seasons.
Spring for blooming.
Summer for thriving.
Autumn for releasing.
Winter for resting.

Where is your body's garden today?

So often, we judge ourselves for being in winter—quiet, low energy, not producing. But winter is not failure.

It is **holy recovery.**

Roots deepen in silence. Soil rests so it can nourish the future.

What if we honored the season we're in, instead of rushing toward a season we think we *should* be in?

You may be in a time of pruning. Growth. Stillness. Anticipation.

All are holy. All belong.

The Garden of Relationships

We don't garden alone.
Even Eden had community.

So ask yourself: **Who is allowed in your garden?**

Who are the sacred companions who water your roots with love?

Who have you allowed to stay in your innermost circle that may no longer belong?

Sometimes we tolerate relationships out of guilt. Other times we guard our gates out of fear. But God invites us into *intentional* community.

Relationships should feel like sunlight: nourishing, warm, and truthful.

Ask yourself:

- Who brings light into your life?
- Who drains your energy?
- Who do you feel safe to be unmasked with?
- Who needs loving boundaries—not as punishment, but as sacred fencing?

You are the steward of your own garden gate.

Fully Present with God

Who in your life feels like nourishing sunlight? Who feels like weeds pulling at your roots?

Your relationships matter. Write down who refreshes you and who drains you. This is not about judgment—it's about awareness.

_____

_____

_____

_____

_____

_____

_____

_____

_____

_____

_____

_____

_____

_____

_____

_____

_____

_____

_____

_____

_____

The Soundscape of the Garden

What sounds fill your inner garden?

Are you surrounded by noise, urgency, distraction?
Or do you hear the birdsong of grace?

Silence is where we often meet God most clearly. But silence can be uncomfortable when we're used to noise.

When you pause—no phone, no tasks, no urgency—what do you hear?

The voice of God is not in the volume.
It is in the tone.
It is loving. Steady. Near.

You might consider a daily practice of stillness—a few minutes each morning to sit with God in your garden and simply *be*.

You don't have to make anything happen.
Eden begins in stillness.

Blessing the Soil

Your garden is not broken.

It is becoming.

Bless the parts of you that feel behind.
Bless the soil that looks barren.
Bless the body that is still healing.

God is not in a rush.
And neither is your soul.

Speak aloud, if you can:

"I bless my mind today.
I bless my breath.
I bless my heart and bones and belly.
I bless my past.
I bless my future.
And I bless this moment I'm in—because God is here, and He calls me good."

Fully Present with God

What do you feel led to bless today in your body, your story, or your relationships?

Maybe it's a scar that reminds you of healing. A friend who stood by you. A season of suffering that grew compassion. Speak blessing over it—naming it as good and holy

_____

_____

_____

_____

_____

_____

_____

_____

_____

_____

_____

_____

_____

_____

_____

_____

_____

_____

_____

_____

_____

Closing Blessing

May you walk slowly through your own garden.
May you listen gently to your breath, your body, your spirit.
May you meet God in your soil today.

In the silence.
In the flow.
In the ache and in the bloom.

May you recognize the voice of God walking with you.
And may you know this above all:

You are not too late.
You are not behind.
You are not failing.
You are not alone.

Your garden is not too far gone.
The Gardener still walks among us.
And He delights in you.

Amen.

Chapter 2

WHO'S TENDING TO YOUR GARDEN

In Eden, man was given purpose. Not just to exist, but to tend. To care. To cultivate.

The very first calling humanity received wasn't to preach, or conquer, or hustle—it was to tend the garden. To nurture life. To participate in creation. And whatever man named, it became.

That kind of authority wasn't domination. It was devotion. It was partnership.

God entrusted Adam with the care of what He had made. He didn't need help—but He wanted it. He wanted to co-create with the one He formed in His image. That same invitation still stands. Not just in Eden, but in you.

So I ask you gently: Who's tending to your garden now?

God the Gardener, You the Partner

Are you open to tending your life with God? Not to impress Him with what you've done in your own strength—but *with* Him?

Humanity often thinks of God as a king we must appease. Bringing gifts like a poor peasant—hoping they are enough. Afraid they won't be.

Jesus doesn't rule like a tyrant. He leads like a servant. He kneels. He washes our feet.

The disciples struggled with this. They expected a Messiah on a warhorse. But they got Love wrapped in skin, kneeling with a towel.

This is the God who says, "Let's tend the garden together."

He walks beside you. He doesn't need your perfection. He wants your presence.

The Creator of the universe wants to co-create with you. Not because you're the most skilled or holy or productive—but because He loves you.

Let that sink in.

Fully Present with God

What would change if you believed God wanted to create with you, not just command you?

Imagine life as co-creation, not performance. How might your body feel different if you lived as God's partner, not His project?

_____

_____

_____

_____

_____

_____

_____

_____

_____

_____

_____

_____

_____

_____

_____

_____

_____

_____

_____

_____

_____

_____

Not a Test. Not a Contest. A Collaboration.

Have you ever felt like life was a test?

That God was the examiner and you were the student trying not to fail?

I lived that way for a long time. Every act felt like a performance. Every failure felt final. Every success felt fragile.

God's love isn't conditional. His presence isn't performance-based.

When I see Him as the co-creator, something shifts. It's no longer pressure—it's presence. No longer duty—it's delight.

He doesn't grade your garden. He gardens *with* you.

He gives seed and water. You provide space and attention. He brings sunlight and grace. You stay present and open.

You don't have to tend your garden alone.

The enemy whispers, *You better not mess this up.*

God's voice says, *Walk with Me. I will do more than you can imagine.*

He doesn't need your performance. He wants your partnership.

The Purpose of the Garden: Loving Stewardship

The role of tending is not managerial. It's relational.

God never asked us to dominate our bodies or our world—but to live in harmony with it. To see the divine in it. To care for it because it is good.

When we tend to something with love, we listen. We notice. We make space for growth and honor each stage of becoming.

So how are you tending to your life? To your body? To your mind? To your emotions? To your inner child?

Are you cultivating space for joy? For rest? For creativity?

Are you pruning what no longer brings life?

God invites us not to conquer our bodies, but to commune with them. Not to master our lives, but to walk with Him as we tend.

Servant Leadership to the Body

Your body is not your slave. It's your sacred partner.

As a physical therapist—and someone who once treated my body like a machine to push, fix, and manage—I've had to unlearn that pattern. My body is not a tool to dominate, but a temple entrusted to me by God.

Now I see myself as a servant leader to my body. Just as Jesus knelt to wash His disciples' feet, I kneel in posture to my body each day. I listen. I support. I allow it to rest. I honor its voice.

That might look like pausing before a meal and asking, *"What will nourish me today?"* It looks like noticing when my body is tired and choosing rest instead of forcing one more task.

It looks like moving—walking, exercising, stretching—not out of punishment, but as a gift to my muscles and lungs. It looks like practicing gratitude for the breath in my chest and the heartbeat I didn't create.

It looks like practicing muscle testing, using the body's natural responses to discern what strengthens or weakens me, allowing my body itself to guide me toward what is good—a simple way of powerfully checking in with God through your body.

If you haven't heard of muscle testing, it's a gentle technique often used in holistic health to "ask" the body what it needs. By applying light pressure to a muscle—often the arm or fingers—you can observe whether the muscle stays strong or weakens in response to a food, thought, or even a question.

It may seem unusual at first, but many people, myself included, have found it to be a surprisingly accurate way of honoring the wisdom God built into our bodies. Think of it as one more way the Spirit partners with us through our design—a way of listening deeply, not only with your mind, but with your body.

This is what servant leadership looks like in the body: listening, tending, honoring. Not pushing, demanding, or silencing.

And it's not so different from servant leadership in the Kingdom. Jesus showed us what it means to lead with humility—He served, He listened, He gave without control or fear.

He washed feet. He broke bread. He welcomed the little ones. He led not by force, but by love.

When I lead my body this way, my body responds—with gratitude, with vitality, with peace.

So ask yourself: Are you leading your body with kindness—or managing it with fear?

God leads us with grace. You are invited to do the same with your body.

The Spirit of Martha: When Responsibility Overrules Relationship

In Scripture, Martha was busy. Doing. Preparing.

Mary sat at Jesus' feet.

I relate to Martha. Maybe you do too.

There's nothing wrong with service.

When it becomes obligation instead of overflow, we miss the moment.

God gently showed me: Even your desire to love others can become distorted when it's not grounded in My love first.

He doesn't shame Martha. He simply invites her to pause.

To sit. To receive. To remember.

Fully Present with God

Where in your life do you feel like you must "prove" your worth to God or others? What would it look like to just sit at Jesus' feet today?

Write about the spaces where striving still drives you. Then imagine simply being with Jesus—no tasks, no achievements—just being loved.

_____

_____

_____

_____

_____

_____

_____

_____

_____

_____

_____

_____

_____

_____

_____

_____

_____

_____

_____

_____

_____

_____

Tending Through Vulnerability

True tending requires honesty.

We can't care for what we pretend doesn't exist. A gardener doesn't ignore the weeds, or the dry soil, or the plants drooping for lack of water. They notice. They name what is true. Then they tend.

It's the same with our bodies and our lives.

Sometimes the bravest act is saying: *I'm not okay today.* Or, *I need help.* Or, *This part of me feels unseen.* That kind of honesty is not weakness— it is sacred strength.

Vulnerability is sacred visibility. It is showing up as we truly are, not as we think we should be. When we stop hiding behind masks of performance, pretending our body is fine when it's crying out for rest, or our spirit is fine when it's aching for connection, we finally create space for healing.

And here's the beauty: when we bring our real selves to God and to others, love can finally reach the places that need it most.

The cracked soil. The shaded corners. The parts of the garden we've kept closed off.

Vulnerability doesn't diminish us. It roots us. It says: This is my real soil. This is where I am. And this is where love can grow.

Fully Present with God

What's one area of your garden you've been afraid to tend? What's waiting to be seen?

It might be your health, your finances, your sexuality, or an old wound. Write the first thing that comes to mind, without censoring it.

_____

_____

_____

_____

_____

_____

_____

_____

_____

_____

_____

_____

_____

_____

_____

_____

_____

_____

Tending Together: Relationships as Co-Gardeners

Who helps you tend your garden?
Who reminds you to rest? To laugh? To hope?
Tending isn't solitary work. It's sacred togetherness.

Sometimes, we need help pulling a weed. Or planting hope. Or remembering joy.

God often sends others—loved ones, friends, mentors, therapists—bearing gifts we uniquely hold for one another, to help us tend to our bodies with love and without judgment.

That last part—*without judgment*—is where discernment begins. Even in our most cherished relationships, we learn to distinguish the voice of love from the voice of fear.

God will speak through those you hold dear.
And still—not every word from them is from Him.

The Father trusts you to feel the difference. To listen. To stay open to the most free, co-creative relationships—those meant to thrive in love and abundance.

You, too, are called to tend others.
Gently. Not by fixing. But by being present.

By bringing the unique voice God placed in you—nourishing others not out of duty, but from the overflow of love.

Pruning: "Cleaning Off"

One of the most sacred practices my wife and I share in stewarding our relationship is what we call *"cleaning off."*

With each other. With God. Our own version of the Trinity.

When a thought, belief, or lingering feeling starts to weigh on us—even if we can't fully name it—we bring it into the light.

It could be something small that happened at work. A tension with a family member. A flare of old hurt or unhealed trauma. An unknown judgement we have against someone.

Sometimes, we don't even know what we're feeling—just that something's off. And so, we clean off.

We pause. We get honest. We invite God in.

Sometimes, it feels like letting go of unspoken anger that's coiled itself around our hearts.

Other times, it's like surfacing something ancient and buried in us— something only the Father could reveal.

But always, *cleaning off* is a return to love. A release of what no longer belongs.

The world tells us to "just let it go."

But this is deeper. This is sacred tending. This is the Father "pruning" us—not with punishment, but with gentle care.

In John 15:2–3, Jesus says the Father prunes the branches *that do bear fruit*—so they may become even more fruitful. He doesn't cast them off. He tends to them. He cleans them.

Immediately after, He says: *"You are already clean because of the word I have spoken to you."*

Religion often reframes pruning as pain—something to brace for. But that doesn't align with how I've experienced the heart of God.

The God I know is infinitely loving.

The Gardener of all creation doesn't slash away with violence. He nurtures. He restores.

So, what if pruning feels more like release? Like someone finally exhaling after days of holding their breath?

Or the deep freedom of weeping in the arms of someone safe while God dissolves a pain you didn't even know you carried?

We've been taught to expect suffering. To brace for discipline.

But maybe... pruning is joy. Maybe it's liberation. That's our experience on the other side of it.

And maybe that's why we now *love* our deep "cleaning off" moments.

They keep secrets out of our marriage. They invite honesty in. They open the door to God's voice—always kind, always healing.

The Father invited me to look at John 15 through His eyes of love—not through fear, not through punishment, but through the lens of divine tending.

Sometimes there are dead beliefs, hurts, or lies still clinging to our branches. And God, in His joy, helps us release them—not to shame us, but to *reveal the true us*.

So I bless you:
To trust the Father's pruning.
To trust the practice of cleaning off.
To trust your own heart and your relationships.
To trust that what God is revealing is always rooted in love.

Let Him clean off what's on you in kindness. Let Him tend to you like a beloved garden. You are being made visible.

Fully Present with God

What would you like to clean off with God? How about with your partner or cherished loved ones?

Think of dirt on the garden tools—resentment, misunderstandings, shame. What needs to be washed clean through honesty, forgiveness, or conversation?

_____

_____

_____

_____

_____

_____

_____

_____

_____

_____

_____

_____

_____

_____

_____

_____

_____

_____

_____

_____

_____

_____

_____

Comparison: The Silent Thief

One of the greatest enemies of our garden is comparison.

I used to think I wasn't doing enough. That others were doing it better. More impact. More obedience. More fruit.

We look at other people's gardens—what they've grown, how fast, how lush—and we begin to judge our own.

Every garden is unique. The flowers that bloom in yours may not even grow in theirs.

The garden God gives you isn't supposed to look like anyone else's. Your soil is different. Your season is different. Your growth is different.

That's the point.

The ground is the same—God's love. But the gifts that sprout? They're uniquely yours.

If we're too busy comparing, we stop cultivating. We leave our garden untended while staring over the fence.

God doesn't ask you to be what humanity calls "the best". He asks you to be *with* Him.

Let this be your gentle reminder: the only garden you're called to tend is yours.

Fully Present with God

Where has comparison crept into your life? How has it affected the way you see your garden?

Be honest. Have you been measuring your body, your gifts, your relationships against someone else's? How does it feel in your spirit when you do?

_____

_____

_____

_____

_____

_____

_____

_____

_____

_____

_____

_____

_____

_____

_____

_____

_____

_____

_____

_____

_____

Closing Blessing

May you know that your garden is worth tending.
May you feel the gentle presence of the Gardener beside you.
May your hands move in love, not fear.
May you rest from the need to prove.

And may you rise each day knowing:
You were never meant to do it all alone.

The Creator of the universe has rolled up His sleeves.
And He is waiting to build something beautiful—with you.

Amen.

Chapter 3

WHERE ARE YOU
IN YOUR GARDEN?

At first glance, "Where are you?" sounds like a question of geography—of location. But in God's hands, it becomes something far deeper. It is less about coordinates on a map and more about the posture of your heart. It is not simply *where you are standing*, but *how you are living*.

Where are you right now?

Where are you—in your breath, in your body, in your spirit?

Not where you want to be.
Not where others think you are.
Not where you pretend to be. But right now.

In Eden, after the fall, God's first question to humanity was this: *Where are you?* He wasn't confused. He didn't lose track of Adam and Eve's location. Instead, He was calling to His beloved children, who had lost track of themselves. They were hiding.

This first question was not for God's sake—but for Adam's. God knew exactly where Adam was.

The question was an invitation: *Do you know where you are? Do you know who you are? Will you trust My voice above the fear that makes you hide?*

God, in His deep love, called to them. And He calls to us still.

Not to shame us.

Not to scold us.

But to draw us home.

Where are you?

This question echoes across the ages, into our present moment, into our hearts and into our bodies.

Are you walking with God in the cool of the day—grounded in abundance, joy, and love?

Or hiding, like Adam and Eve, wrapped in fig leaves of fear and shame?

Maybe you're all over the place. Most of us are. And that's okay.

This chapter is about sacred orientation. About re-locating ourselves in truth, in awareness, in love.

Walking with God in Abundance, Joy, and Love?

There are days when we know exactly where we are.

We feel it in our bones: *I am walking with God.*

I am aware of His voice, His presence, His joy. I am in sync with the Spirit.

These are sacred days. Days where love feels real, not just an idea. Where peace isn't something we chase, but something that holds us.

If that's where you are—receive it. Let it fill you.

Don't be surprised when other days come.

Hiding in Fear and Shame?

There are days we want to hide. Days we do hide. From people. From our pain. Even from ourselves.

We numb, we deflect, we distract. Sometimes we're not hiding because we think we're evil.

We're hiding because we're scared. Ashamed. Disoriented.

God never stops calling. Not with a shout, but with a whisper. Not with judgment, but with love.

"Where are you?"

It's not an interrogation. It's an invitation. To name where we really are. To stop pretending. To be found.

Or All Over the Place?

Sometimes, the truth is: we're a mix.

A little joy. A little fear. A little peace. A little panic.

We're tending the garden and hiding in the weeds. We're human.

God meets us right there, in the complexity.

He doesn't need you to clean up to be found. He just needs honesty.

"Here I am, Lord. Scattered. And here."

Fully Present with God

Where are you today? Emotionally? Physically? Spiritually? Can you name it without self-judgment?

Write what's true—even if it's tired, anxious, numb, or joyful. The act of naming is an act of love.

_____

_____

_____

_____

_____

_____

_____

_____

_____

_____

_____

_____

_____

_____

_____

_____

_____

_____

_____

_____

_____

_____

A Loving God Seeking Relationship

Where are you? is the call of connection. It's the heart of a loving Parent who wants you to be present with Him again.

No matter where you are—confused, anxious, lost, angry, numb—He comes walking in the garden. Not yelling. Just looking. Just asking.

"Where are you, Beloved? I miss you."

God doesn't need GPS. He's God and is already in our garden. But He invites us to locate ourselves—not so we can earn love—but so we can return to love.

He keeps asking, not because He doesn't know, but because we forget to ask ourselves.

The True North Star

God's voice is the ultimate orientation point. The North Star for our journey.

In the Christmas story, people followed a literal star.

Wise men, travelers, watchers of the sky—they trusted a light to lead them. And it did. It led them to the miraculous, the Savior.

How beautiful that the redemption of Eden began with people turning toward a light. A reversal of the original story, where humanity turned away from light and love.

God's voice isn't just truth. It's direction. When we don't know the way forward, we listen for the One who made the path.

His voice doesn't push. It pulls. It draws us gently, like gravity to light.

Where Are You, Really?

Drowning? I've been there. In every way.

In *The River*, I drowned and met God—literally.

Before and after that moment, I was drowning slowly in other ways: pressure, fear, exhaustion, performance.

Are you drowning now? Financially? Emotionally? Spiritually?

Are you pushing through something that was meant to be soft? Are you surviving in something that was meant to be sacred?

God knows. And He asks not to expose you, but to orient you.

Because until we admit where we are, we can't take a step forward.

Land Navigation 101

I served in the military. In land navigation, the first and most vital step before moving toward your goal is knowing exactly where you are.

Skip that step, and you'll wander in circles, wasting time, burning out, or worse—ending up further from where you were meant to go.

You can't reach your destination if you don't know where you're starting from. That first starting coordinate? It matters most.

Otherwise, every step you take—even if you're moving fast—is in the wrong direction.

I've had those moments. Feeling lost. Spinning in circles. Refusing to admit it. And only getting more disoriented.

It wasn't until I stopped, got honest, and said, "I have no idea where I am," that I could be found.

It's the same spiritually.

You can't walk forward in faith until you're honest about where you're standing.

It may be in a dark valley. It may be in joy. It may be somewhere in between. But truth brings light.

God never shamed Adam for his answer. He simply invited him into a deeper conversation. The truth is the doorway to grace.

God isn't afraid of your confusion. He just wants you to stop running and be honest.

"Here I am. I don't know where I am. And I want to find You."

He will help you find Him and you.

Fully Present with God

Imagine God saying your name right now. Not in anger. In pure, infinite love. What does that voice feel like? What is it drawing you toward?

Write down what you hear, see, or sense in that moment. Does His voice invite you to rest, to trust, to hope again?

_____

_____

_____

_____

_____

_____

_____

_____

_____

_____

_____

_____

_____

_____

_____

_____

_____

_____

_____

_____

Lost in New Places

It's one thing to be lost in a city or a training ground. It's another thing to feel lost in your own skin. In your own story. In your own mind.

Those are the moments when we need the gentlest voice. The kindest light.

That's what God offers. Not a map. A presence.

He doesn't always give step-by-step directions.

Sometimes, He just says your name. And that's enough to turn us home.

The Disoriented Body

Sometimes we feel lost in our minds. Sometimes we feel lost in our bodies.

Fatigue. Chronic pain. A sense of disconnection.

These aren't just physical issues.

They're location signals from the garden within.

"Where are you?" might sound like:

- Where is your breath today?
- Where is your joy?
- Where is your center?

Disorientation often shows up somatically:

- Shallow breathing
- Tension in the shoulders
- Brain fog
- Tight jaw
- Racing heart

These are not failures. They are invitations. God does not push us to fix. He invites us to listen.

The Hidden Garden: When You've Gone Numb

Sometimes we don't feel anything at all. Not joy. Not sadness. Not pain. Not hope.

This, too, is a location. Numbness is not absence.

If that's where you are—if your garden feels frozen, barren, or dull— take heart.

Even in the coldest winter, roots are growing.

Even in numbness, God is present.

He does not rush spring. He simply stays close to you, warms the soil, and waits with us.

Fully Present with God

Where in your body are you feeling discomfort, tightness, silence, or numbness? What might that part be trying to say?

Place your hand there. Breathe. Listen. Don't rush to fix—simply let that part of your body speak.

_____

_____

_____

_____

_____

_____

_____

_____

_____

_____

_____

_____

_____

_____

_____

_____

_____

_____

_____

_____

_____

_____

Orientation Restores Dignity

When we orient ourselves in truth, we reclaim our power.

Not power over others, but the power to move forward honestly.

The world says you need a map. Heaven says you need to pause and listen.

Orientation is a sacred pause.

It's the moment we sit under a tree and breathe.

It's the moment we stop running in unnecessary haste.

It's the moment we realize: we were never lost to Him.

Even when we don't feel found, we are.

Whose Voice are You Orienting To?

Whose voice is shaping your orientation?

- Is it the voice of fear?
- The voice of urgency?
- The voice of comparison?
- Or is it the voice of God?

The voice of fear disorients. It pulls us away from truth and scatters us in every direction:

- "There's no way I'm going to pay my bills."
- "I'll never be enough."
- "If I stop striving, I'll lose everything."

The voice of God—always the voice of love—reorients. It grounds us in peace, abundance, and belonging:

- "I will supply all your needs according to My riches in glory."
- "You are My beloved child, wonderfully made."
- "Be still and know that I am God; you don't have to carry this alone."

72

God's voice is not the loudest, but it is always the most loving. He will not shame you for where you are. He will gently call you by name and bring you back to center.

Where are you, Beloved?

Are you near still waters?

Clinging to the edge?

Curled up under the fig leaves of old beliefs?

Are you racing through your garden, too afraid to stop?

There's no wrong answer. There's only presence.

Healing Begins With Orientation

The healing didn't start when Adam was removed from Eden. It started the moment he answered. The moment he came out of hiding.

Healing doesn't demand perfection. It begins with acknowledgment.

Orientation is not arrival. It's not victory. It's just the holy first step.

Where are you, friend? And are you willing to be found?

Closing Blessing

May you hear the loving question today.
May you not be afraid to answer honestly.
May your location become your liberation.
May your truth open the gate to healing.
And may the One who walks in gardens walk with you.
Wherever you are.

Amen.

Chapter 4

HOW IS THE FRUIT IN YOUR GARDEN?

There is something deeply sacred about fruit. It is both result and revelation. It reflects the nature of the seed, the quality of the soil, and the presence of sunlight and water.

Fruit doesn't lie. It tells the truth of what is growing, how it's growing, and what it's connected to.

Think about the last time you tasted fruit picked straight from a garden or orchard—warm from the sun, bursting with juice, alive with sweetness.

Now compare that to fruit that's sat for weeks on a store shelf: duller in color, tougher in skin, less vibrant in flavor.

Both are "fruit," but only one carries the fullness of life.

Good fruit reveals good seed, tended in love, nourished in light, rooted in fertile soil. Weak fruit reveals what's been disconnected, neglected, or forced.

I ask with love, not pressure: How is the fruit in your garden?

This is not a performance question. It is a presence question.

A Divine Inventory

We are going to take an inventory as a way to assess the fruit. This isn't about performance, but about presence—looking inward at the beautiful fruit God has planted within us. Just like walking through a garden to notice what is ripening, what needs more sunlight, or what may need pruning, we're going to pause and see what's growing in the garden of our hearts.

Let's not take this inventory with shame or guilt. We don't measure the garden with a red pen or harsh voice.

We listen. We notice. We receive.

What is growing in you right now? Is it love? Peace? Patience? Or maybe frustration, fear, or fatigue?

There's no pass/fail here. Only observation. Let's walk the rows together.

The Fruits of the Spirit and Beyond

In Scripture, we are given a list of what the Spirit produces in us: love, joy, peace, patience, kindness, goodness, faithfulness, gentleness, and self-control. These are not rules. They are fruits—natural outcomes of divine presence.

These are not the only fruits that grow in our gardens. Boldness, curiosity, creativity, wonder—these, too, are gifts of the Spirit. They just didn't make the list. And they matter.

The enemy would love to twist this truth. To make fruit into religion. To make every garden into a factory that looks just like another.

God plants unique seeds in each of us.

And only He knows what fruits are meant to flourish in your garden.

Asking Your Body

Ask your body: *How are the fruits in my garden?*

Pause. Notice what arises.

Do you feel a sense of clarity, a soft peace, a gentle "yes" deep within? Or does your body feel tight, heavy, or restless? Both are invitations. Both are ways God speaks.

Start with love. Once you have tended to love, we'll move together to the next fruits—joy, peace, and beyond. One by one, we'll walk the garden, listening for what is ready to bloom.

Lean into the voice of your body. Be still and intentional—allow space for your body to speak before your mind rushes in.

Let your chest rise, let your breath flow, and simply listen.

What is your body saying about love? Begin here, with love first, for it is the soil in which every other fruit grows.

Is love flourishing and flowing, nourished by the light of the Father? Or is it torn, wilted, clinging to the last petal?

I have been there—unsure that love would ever bloom again. Believing I wasn't worthy. That love was for other gardens, not mine.

That is a lie.

Love is your birthright.

It was and is the first fruit. And it still grows. Even in the dark. Even under heavy clouds. If God gave it to you, you are worthy of it.

Love: The Foundational Fruit

Love is the sunbeam that nurtures all other fruit.

Not performance-based love. Not approval-seeking love. Not "I'll be worthy when" love.

The love that says: *You are already mine. You are already worthy. You are already beloved.*

Is love growing in your garden?

Even one bloom of love can fill your entire garden with fragrance. Even one seed, watered gently with truth, will grow.

Fully grown vibrant love, grounded in the Father's love is enough to change the world.

You are loved, let love flourish in your garden and watch what you and God will do!

Fully Present with God

Where are you seeing love grow in your life? Where might it need more light? Who is the source of the grounding love in your life? Are you open to infinite love being the root of every fruit that grows—forever?

Reflect on the places where love is strong—and the places it feels starved. Then picture God's infinite love as sunlight pouring over every branch.

_____

_____

_____

_____

_____

_____

_____

_____

_____

_____

_____

_____

_____

_____

_____

_____

_____

_____

_____

Joy and Peace: The Wind Through the Trees

Joy is the sound of laughter echoing through the orchard. Peace is the stillness in the soil.

Are these fruits growing in your garden? Or have they been choked out by comparison, pressure, or busyness?

Is joy like dancing sunflowers in the breeze?

Or has it felt buried under the weight of life?

Even if all seems lost: there is still a seed. One seed of joy can change the whole field.

And peace?

Peace isn't the absence of problems. It's the presence of God in the midst of them.

What would it look like to nourish your peace like a tender vine, not a goal to achieve?

Patience, Kindness, Goodness: The Relational Harvest

These fruits often grow in how we interact with others—and ourselves.

Are you patient with your own process?

Are you kind to your body, your emotions, your past?

Do you see patience as painfully waiting—or as joyfully experiencing the present moment while drawing in an abundant future?

Is goodness something you practice toward yourself, or something you believe is reserved only for others?

Our bodies respond to kindness. Our nervous systems settle when we are gentle with ourselves. Our immune systems thrive in environments of love.

These fruits flourish in love, not performance.

I used to try to muscle my way into goodness, thinking if I just did enough good, I'd finally be good.

The fruit didn't ripen that way. It soured in performance. It ripened in grace.

Sometimes, hiding these fruits exposes the pain beneath.

I have hidden these fruits before, afraid to look "odd" in a world that prizes sarcasm over sincerity.

These fruits are cherished. They nourish others. They nourish you.

Fully Present with God

What fruit do you feel pressured to hide or ignore because it doesn't match what others value?

Is it gentleness in a world that prizes hustle? Creativity in a culture that prizes logic? Write what you've been tempted to hide and ask God how He sees it.

_____

_____

_____

_____

_____

_____

_____

_____

_____

_____

_____

_____

_____

_____

_____

_____

_____

_____

_____

_____

_____

Kindness to Self

Let's pause here.

Are you kind to yourself?

I used to think kindness to self was selfish. That putting myself last was holy.

God is showing me something different.

That when I am gentle with myself, I become a better steward of the garden. That self-hatred poisons the soil.

That self-love, grounded in God's love, multiplies the fruit for others.

Fully Present with God

What does kindness from you to you look like this week?

A nap? A walk? A meal you enjoy? Write something small and tangible—and give it to yourself like a gift.

_____

_____

_____

_____

_____

_____

_____

_____

_____

_____

_____

_____

_____

_____

_____

_____

_____

_____

_____

_____

Faithfulness and Self-Control

These fruits have been weaponized.

I saw them as obligation. As pressure. As effort I had to muster.

True faithfulness flows from trust.

Self-control isn't about suppression. It's about identity.

When I know who I am, and Whose I am, I don't have to grasp or force goodness.

God's glory and our joy are not opposites! They are aligned.

The enemy wants you to believe joy is sin. That fun is failure.

The Father invites you into joy. Come share in your Father's joy, Jesus said.

Let love be the foundation for these fruits, and watch self-honoring practices bloom with ease—no longer choked by the weight of obligation.

The Fruit We Don't Talk About

Sometimes we grow things not listed in Galatians 5. Things like:

- Boldness
- Creativity
- Curiosity
- Rest
- Play
- Humor
- Imagination
- Openness

These, too, are fruits.

Your unique garden may grow fruits no one has ever tasted before. That doesn't make them less holy. It makes them part of the divine mosaic.

God delights in the originality of His children.

For one, the fruit may be the ability to plan years ahead with wisdom and foresight—seeing patterns and preparing paths that others cannot.

For another, it may be the gift of connecting instantly with people, creating a sense of safety and belonging wherever they go.

Some may carry the fruit of being fully attuned to their body, able to sense what brings health and what does not, guiding others into deeper wholeness.

Others may carry laughter that heals a room, or a quiet presence that steadies storms.

The fruit in your life might be different from your neighbor's—and it is blessed, sacred, and full of purpose.

God doesn't ask for sameness. He delights in the variety, the originality, and the way each fruit reflects His goodness in a unique way.

Think of a garden where no two flowers are alike—roses, lilies, daisies, and wildflowers all growing side by side.

Each contributes to the beauty of the whole, not by competing, but by simply being what they were created to be. In the same way, your fruit—no matter how unusual or uncommon—is a vital part of God's abundant garden.

Fully Present with God

What unique fruits has God planted in your life that may not look like anyone else's? Are you allowing them to grow? How can you celebrate them?

Write the quirks, passions, or talents that make you unique. Thank God for them. They are holy seeds.

_____

_____

_____

_____

_____

_____

_____

_____

_____

_____

_____

_____

_____

_____

_____

_____

_____

_____

_____

_____

_____

_____

_____

Daily Fruit Checks: A Gentle Practice

Taking inventory of the fruit in your garden doesn't have to be complicated. It can be as natural as breathing, a rhythm that begins in the morning and closes with reflection at night.

In the Morning

When you rise, pause before rushing into the day. Place your hand on your heart and ask: *What fruit is ripe in me today?*

It may be joy, rising like the sun, giving you strength to face what's ahead.

It may be love, calling you to nurture your family, your work, or even yourself with tenderness.

It may simply be courage—the quiet bravery to get out of bed and take one small step forward.

In the Evening

As you lay your head down, take a moment to reflect: *Where did I see the Spirit move through me today?*

Was there an abundance of love in the way you spoke to someone who needed encouragement?

Did joy surprise you in laughter you didn't expect?

Did peace anchor you in a moment that could have felt overwhelming?

Did patience or kindness bloom in your interactions, even when the day was hard?

When You Feel Out of Sync

If at any point you feel scattered or disconnected, gently ask: *What does my soil need?*

Perhaps your spirit is thirsty for rest.

Perhaps your body is asking for movement, or your heart for quiet connection with God.

Listen without judgment. Your garden flourishes not by striving, but by receiving the right care at the right time.

This isn't performance. It's presence.

Let this practice become a daily rhythm of awareness—beginning and ending in love, rooted in God's voice, and overflowing with the fruit He has already planted in you.

Closing Blessing

May you walk gently among your trees today.
May you see with soft eyes what is blooming.

May you experience patience in the pace of your fruit.
May you give grace to what is not yet ripe.

May you and the Lord enjoy the first fruits of your garden together.
May your garden reflect heaven in your own unique way.
And may you delight in the fruit that only your garden was designed to grow.

Amen.

Chapter 5

HOW IS THE VIBRANCY OF YOUR GARDEN?

Picture a beautiful garden in full bloom. The soil is rich, the leaves are deep green, blossoms open wide, and fruit hangs heavy on the branches. The air hums with bees and the quiet buzz of life.

A vibrant garden is not just surviving—it is flourishing. It is full of movement, color, light, and flow.

So it is with our inner garden.

Just as a physical garden reveals its health through lushness, strength, and fruitfulness, our bodies and spirits reveal their vibrancy in how we feel, move, and live.

Vibrancy is not perfection—it is aliveness.

It's the felt sense that your body, your being, your soul are flowing with divine energy. It is resilience, joy, peace, and strength moving through you like living water.

Your body, too, is a garden. Designed by a loving Creator. Entrusted to you as a sacred space where spirit and matter, heaven and earth, meet in beautiful connection.

This chapter is where we gather everything we've explored so far and bring it into embodied practice.

Because a garden is not just meant to be admired—it's meant to be walked through, tended, and enjoyed.

Let's check in on the vibrancy of your garden.

Yes—it gets to be simple. It gets to be easy. It gets to be full of grace.

So how is the vibrancy of your garden?

Not just the presence of fruit. The quality of your soil.

Not just how your body moves. How it feels. Not just survival. Aliveness.

Let's explore how vibrancy lives in our physical bodies, in the unseen energy of our lives, and in the way we listen to the voice of God in our cells.

Are You Open to More Than One Way?

So many of us split things apart:

- Science vs. spirituality
- Religion vs. medicine
- Eastern vs. Western
- Head vs. heart

What if healing was in the space between?

Jesus didn't come to pick human sides. He came to make people whole.

The moment we lock ourselves into one belief system and reject all else, we may miss the healing God has placed just across the room.

One of my favorite sci-fi characters once warned, *"Only a Sith deals in absolutes."*
The wisdom is real.

In the Star Wars universe, the Sith represent an evil sect that reduces everything to extremes—light or dark, good or bad, all or nothing. But life with God is not confined to such rigid categories. It is full of nuance, mystery, and infinite colors—like the countless shades that make up creation and the vast universe itself.

In the same way, God's voice doesn't bind us to harsh absolutes or rigid formulas. He speaks in love, in presence, in whispers that invite us deeper into relationship.

While fear shouts in black-and-white terms—*you'll never make it, you'll always fail, you have to choose one or the other*—the Spirit of God opens us to possibilities we could never imagine on our own. His voice breathes freedom, creativity, and grace into the garden of our lives.

If you feel stuck in your health—physically, emotionally, spiritually— maybe the next step is simply to ask: *Am I open to healing coming from somewhere I don't expect?*

Fully Present with God

Is there a belief you hold tightly about wellness or healing that may be limiting you from receiving more?

For example: *Healing takes forever. I'll always be sick. My family history defines me.* Write the beliefs—and then imagine releasing them like weeds pulled from the soil.

_____

_____

_____

_____

_____

_____

_____

_____

_____

_____

_____

_____

_____

_____

_____

_____

_____

_____

_____

_____

_____

_____

Check-In #1: Meditation & Body Inquiry

What happens when you pause and ask your body how it's doing?

Not with fear. With loving leadership.

Find a quiet space. Breathe. Ask, *Body, how are you today?*

What do you need from me?

Sometimes your body will speak with tightness.
Sometimes with a memory.
Sometimes just with a sigh of relief that you're finally listening.

I didn't realize how much I treated my body like a machine—until I started listening.

I was more dictator than gardener. I pushed harder, demanded more, ignored the signals, and silenced its voice. No wonder my body rebelled.

That rebellion showed up as sickness, fatigue, lingering injuries, brain fog, pain, and a constant sense that my body was betraying me. It felt like my body was working against me, wearing down faster than it should.

When I shifted from control to care, everything began to change. Under loving leadership, my body started to flourish. The rebellion turned into renewal.

Today, I see the fruit of that partnership: slowed aging, a more youthful appearance, steady energy, mental clarity, vitality that overflows into my work and relationships, and a joy that radiates from within.

What once felt like a battlefield has become a garden of abundant health—full of strength, grace, and life.

Check-In #2: Medicine in ALL Its Forms

I've worked in healthcare for nearly two decades. I've also sat with spiritual leaders, natural healers, and functional medicine practitioners.

Here's the truth: God is not limited to one modality.

He can use the surgeon and the shaman. The pill and the prayer. The data and the divine.

Are you open to being healed by someone who doesn't even believe in God?

He can use anyone. Anything.

So many are waiting for a miracle and rejecting the methods God already sent.

Do you want to be "right"? Or do you want to be well?

Fully Present with God

Is there a method or system of healing you've dismissed that may actually hold something for you?

It could be therapy, prayer, meditation, rest, or even a new way of eating. Write with openness.

_____

Check-In #3: Exercise Response

Exercise is vital. But so is the way we exercise.

Are you moving your body out of love? Or fear?

Movement in love looks like joy, freedom, and flow—dancing barefoot in the kitchen, walking at the pace of gratitude, stretching to release tension, or exercising to celebrate what your body can do.

Movement in fear, on the other hand, often feels like punishment: pushing yourself because you're afraid of weight gain, forcing another rep to prove your worth, or avoiding movement entirely because you fear failure, pain, or not measuring up.

As a physical therapist, I saw both extremes. Some patients pushed their bodies past their limits—driven by fear, perfectionism, or comparison.

Their bodies bore the cost: stress fractures, overuse injuries, chronic pain, and even illness rooted in exhaustion.

Others did the opposite—they avoided movement altogether. Out of fear of pain, fear of failure, or sheer neglect, they starved their bodies of the stimulation they were designed for. This, too, created suffering: weakness, stiffness, disease, and the quiet loss of function over time.

Your body needs movement. But it also needs mercy.

Some days it asks for fire—strength, power, sweat. Some days it asks for water—gentle stretching, a slow walk, rest that heals.

Flexibility, not rigidity, is the mark of a loving leader.

When you listen to your body with love instead of fear, movement becomes not a demand but a gift—a way of honoring the sacred garden you've been entrusted with.

Check-In #4: Elimination (Yes, Pooping)

Let's talk about it.

Are you releasing what doesn't serve you?

Your body is designed to eliminate. Regularly. Cleanly. Without shame.

Society treats this sacred process as gross, embarrassing, or inappropriate.

Could you—or someone you love—be holding onto something that no longer belongs? The Father gently calls us to release all that no longer serves, so we can make space for what is truly meant to remain.

Waste. Trauma. Pain. All things that get to pass through our bodies, unless WE want to cling to them.

Toxicity in our gut, our digestive system, and our body as a whole reshapes the entire landscape of our garden.

The soil of our inner Eden matters. When it's polluted, everything we try to grow—our energy, our joy, our relationships—feels weighed down.

The gut is more than just a place where food is broken down; it's one of the central hubs of our health. Scientists now talk about the *gut–brain connection*—the way imbalances in our digestive system can affect mood, clarity, and even anxiety or depression.

A toxic gut can throw hormones off balance, drain our energy, cloud our thinking, and create inflammation that seeps into every corner of our lives.

I've seen it in my own body and in the lives of those I've walked with—how what's happening in the gut shows up everywhere else: fatigue that feels endless, irritability that seems unexplainable, brain fog that dulls creativity, even chronic pain or disease that feels like it comes from nowhere.

Our inner garden is constantly speaking to us, and the gut is often its loudest voice.

And yet—when our gut is flowing the way God designed, when our bodies eliminate what no longer serves us, there's a deep freedom.

Let me tell you—when you or someone you love struggles to eliminate waste, you realize just how holy this function is.

Pooping is praise. It's the body saying, *I'm free of what I no longer need.*

So can we stop shaming our own biology? Can we bless what God calls good?

Fully Present with God

How is your poop? Is it regular and flowing? Is it constipated and backed up? Is it a source of embarrassment? And in the same way, how is the releasing of things that don't belong both physically and emotionally?

Don't laugh this off—your gut tells the truth. Write honestly. Your body's ability to release is holy, not shameful.

_____

_____

_____

_____

_____

_____

_____

_____

_____

_____

_____

_____

_____

_____

_____

_____

_____

_____

_____

Check-In #5: Your Systems

Let's take a moment to walk through your garden's systems:

- Brain & Nervous System
- Eyes, Ears, and Senses
- Cells & Organs
- Muscles, Bones, Joints
- Digestive System
- Lymphatic & Fluid System
- Metabolic & Endocrine System
- Immune System
- Cardiovascular & Pulmonary Systems
- Skin & Hair

Ask:

- What's going well?
- What needs attention?
- What might God be pointing to gently today?

Healing starts with noticing. And sometimes God will whisper an answer that sits on the other side of your certainty.

Fully Present with God

Which part of your body needs your loving attention today? What is it asking for?

Your back? Your eyes? Your stomach? Put your hand there. Write what comes to mind as you listen.

Tending with Curiosity, Not Judgment

Vibrancy thrives under care, not critique.

It's easy to fall into self-surveillance. To treat our body like a broken machine needing constant repair.

Your garden doesn't need a tyrant. It needs a gardener.

A tender, curious one.

A childlike gardener with a beginner's mindset. Willing to learn what makes it flourish.

Vibrancy comes when we return to the posture of listening.

To what our bodies need.

To what our souls are speaking.

To what God is whispering in the still, small movements of our breath.

Fully Present with God

Where have you been judging your body instead of tending to it?
Be specific. Is it weight, appearance, pain, or function? How could you
tend with compassion instead of criticism?

_____

_____

_____

_____

_____

_____

_____

_____

_____

_____

_____

_____

_____

_____

_____

_____

_____

_____

_____

_____

_____

_____

A Symphony of Systems: Listening to the Whole Garden

Your garden has many systems—each one essential, each one with its own rhythm, and all designed to work in harmony like a divine symphony. When one section is out of tune, the whole song feels off. But when each part plays its role, beauty flows through your whole being.

Think of it this way:

- **Your nervous system is the wind that moves the trees.** It stirs every branch, sending signals that ripple through your body. Just like the wind can whisper gently or roar with force, your nervous system can calm or overwhelm depending on how it's tended.
- **Your digestive system is the soil where nutrients absorb.** Rich soil grows life; depleted soil struggles to sustain it. What you put into your body, and how well your gut breaks it down, determines the richness of what grows.
- **Your circulatory system is the river that waters the roots.** With every beat of your heart, life-giving blood flows, carrying oxygen and nutrients to every cell. A free-flowing river nourishes the whole garden. A blocked river leaves parts of the land dry and struggling.
- **Your immune system is the entryway to the garden, defending the gate.** It's the watchman on the wall, discerning what belongs and what doesn't. When it's strong and balanced, the garden thrives. When it's overwhelmed or distracted, intruders slip in and harm the growth.

Every day, your body plays this symphony—sometimes smooth, sometimes dissonant.

The sounds of your garden might be the sigh of relief when stress leaves your chest, the growl of hunger reminding you of your needs, or the steady rhythm of your breath grounding you in the present.

Vibrancy comes not just when these systems are functioning, but when they are communicating—when the wind, soil, river, and gatekeeper all work together in God's design.

That's when the inner Eden becomes alive with flow, harmony, and peace.

Many of us were taught to ignore these systems until they scream.

God designed them to whisper.

- A tension in the neck might mean a truth you're not speaking.
- Bloating may mean a boundary you're not setting.
- Low energy may be a sacred nudge to rest.

Your body doesn't betray you. It speaks for you. Are you listening?

The Role of Movement in Vibrancy

Movement isn't just exercise. It's aliveness.

A vibrant garden sways. It stretches. It breathes.

We were never meant to be still all the time. Nor were we meant to grind through constant output.

We were made to flow.

What does joyful movement look like for you?

- A walk with a friend
- Dancing in your living room
- Stretching slowly at dawn
- Playing tag with your children

Movement releases the waters of vibrancy. It tells the body: *I am alive, and I am safe.*

Rest: The Unseen Root of Radiance

Nothing blooms all the time.

Rest is not the opposite of vibrancy. It is its foundation.

In rest, the roots grow deeper. The soil restores. The unseen work unfolds.

We live in a world that praises over-striving—but your garden was designed to flourish in holy rhythm.

Sleep. Silence. Sabbath. These are not luxuries. They are life.

Jesus napped in the boat during a storm. God rested on the seventh day. Your body, too, deserves the precious pause.

We continue exploring the importance of rest in Chapter 7.

Watering the Garden: Nourishment and Delight

What are you feeding your body? Not just food—but messages. Environment. Connection. Creativity.

Vibrancy doesn't come from counting calories or strict control. It flows from honoring what your body asks for.

Nourishment can look like:

- A meal made with love and shared in peace
- Music that makes your cells sing
- A conversation that leaves you feeling more alive
- A quiet walk where you finally exhale

Delight is a nutrient. God made us for enjoyment. Eden was filled with beauty and fruit.

You are allowed to feel good. You are allowed to savor.

Fully Present with God

What kind of nourishment is your body craving right now?
It could be food, sunlight, water, movement, or rest. Write it down—
and see if you can honor that craving today.

_____

_____

_____

_____

_____

_____

_____

_____

_____

_____

_____

_____

_____

_____

_____

_____

_____

_____

_____

_____

_____

_____

Vibrancy and the Voice of the Spirit

Vibrancy isn't only physical. It's spiritual alignment. When we're walking in step with the Spirit, we feel more spacious. More clear. More us.

Are you moving with God's rhythm or someone else's?

When the Spirit flows freely in us, vibrancy follows. It's not forced. It's fruit.

So pause. Breathe. Ask:

- What pace is God inviting me to walk at today?
- What energy is He breathing into this moment?

Let your spirit lead the way.

Closing Blessing

May you see your body as a whole, vibrant garden.
May you bless every system, every signal, every sensation.
May you release shame and everything that doesn't belong.
May healing flow to you from every direction and may the Spirit show you how to receive it.

May your garden hum with the music of life.
May joy move through your limbs.
May the Spirit breathe vibrancy into your soil.

And may you remember: your body was made not just to survive, but to radiate.

You are not a machine. You are a miracle.
And your vibrancy matters to the One who made you.

Amen.

Chapter 6

THE "SECRET" SYSTEMS IN YOUR GARDEN

S ome systems in your garden are rarely talked about. Not because they are unimportant, but because the world has labeled them too messy, too shameful, too inappropriate to bring into the open.

These are the **secret systems**—the places we often keep quiet about even with those closest to us.

Think about it: topics like sexual wellness, money, grief, anger, even how we steward our time—these can all trigger discomfort, fear, or shame.

They touch deep places of vulnerability. Many of us were raised to avoid them in polite conversation, or worse, to hide how we're really doing even from our spouses, families, and closest friends.

And that silence doesn't protect us—it seeds separation. It isolates us from each other, and it distances us from the healing voice of God.

But God does not shy away from the secret spaces. In fact, these are often the very places He most longs to enter with His love. The areas we've been told to hide are the very ones where His Spirit can bring the deepest freedom, wholeness, and joy.

Your secret systems matter. They are not dirty, unholy, or too far gone. They are sacred. And they are worthy of tending—worthy of being brought into the light of God's presence.

So in this chapter, let's open the book on these hidden systems.

Let's walk through them with vulnerability, courage, and grace.

Let's invite God into the places we've been taught to lock away, and allow Him to show us that what the world calls shameful, He calls redeemable.

Sexuality: Naked and Unashamed

Do you believe God cares about your sexual wellness?

Really think about it.

Most of us have been taught—directly or subtly—that parts of our bodies are shameful. That sex is taboo. That certain desires must be hidden.

In the beginning, Adam and Eve were naked and unashamed.

Before shame entered the garden, vulnerability was the norm.

We've been taught to treat sexual wellness as something to hush or hide—to feel guilt for what was designed by a loving Creator.

Sexual wellness is spiritual wellness.

It's about more than intercourse. It's about:

- Connection
- Creativity
- Receptivity
- Vulnerability
- Joy

God formed your reproductive system with beauty and intention. He called it good. Very good.

There were no exceptions.

So how is the sexual wellness of your garden today?

Do you treat your body with sacred respect? Are you open to joy, play, vulnerability, intimacy? Are you walking with a partner who shares that same openness?

Most importantly—have you invited God into this space?

Not to judge, but to bless. To laugh with you. To guide you. To show you what love looks like in and out of the bedroom.

Yes, God is that intimate. Yes, He is playful. Yes, He is present.

Sexual wellness in the garden means freedom. Not just freedom from shame—but freedom to explore love without fear. To see your body as beautiful, whole, and sacred.

In a relationship rooted in God's love, sexual intimacy becomes spiritual intimacy. It becomes a place of play, of laughter, of connection. Not a place of guilt or fear.

If you're single, this conversation still matters. Your sexual system is not only for another—it is for your own wholeness. Your own understanding. Your own stewardship.

When we welcome God into our sexual wellness, He doesn't recoil. He draws near. He smiles. He celebrates.

He wants your whole garden vibrant.

Fully Present with God

What would it look like to invite God into your understanding of sexual wellness? Where do you need more freedom?

Write honestly—even if it feels messy. God already knows. Invite Him into what has been hidden.

_____

_____

_____

_____

_____

_____

_____

_____

_____

_____

_____

_____

_____

_____

_____

_____

_____

_____

_____

_____

_____

_____

Money: Butterflies in the Garden

Money, like butterflies, was always meant to move freely—light, beautiful, and life-giving as it flutters through the garden. In a healthy garden, butterflies aren't hoarded or caged.

They come and go, pollinating, spreading beauty, bringing balance, and reminding us of abundance.

I see money in the same way.

It was never meant to be chained down by fear or control. It was meant to flow, to circulate, to bless.

To be admired like beauty in the garden, not clutched like a possession we're terrified to lose.

And yet, how do you feel about money?

For many of us, the answer is complicated. Fear. Shame. Anxiety.

Maybe you grew up without enough and learned to cling tightly to every dollar. Maybe you were taught to view wealth with suspicion, or even to believe the lie that money itself is evil.

But what if money, like the butterflies, was always meant to be free?

Let's go deeper.

God isn't afraid of wealth. In fact, Scripture is filled with stories of stewards, kings, and providers—people entrusted with abundance.

Money is not evil. The idolization of money, as the idolization of anything, can be the root of all kinds of evil. And the fear of money can be just as damaging.

Do you trust yourself with provision? Do you trust God to guide you?

I used to believe having too much would pull me away from heaven. Now I believe I am welcoming the abundance of heaven into every space I enter—including finance.

Wealth can look like butterflies fluttering through a thriving garden.

Are there many flowers—many streams of income—for them to land on?

Or are you clinging to a single vine, praying it's enough?

In your garden, money is not the master. It can be a beautiful butterfly. That responds to:

- Peaceful ground
- Open-handedness
- Flow, not control

Financial health is spiritual health. How we handle money often reveals how we handle trust.

Are you holding too tightly because you fear lack?

Are you reckless because you fear being seen as controlling or controlled?

Are you detached because it feels unholy to manage something called "evil"?

God wants your provision to flow freely. Like joy. Like love. Like water.

He multiplies loaves. He provides taxes from a fish. He honors stewardship—not scarcity.

You can walk in abundance without shame. You can desire overflow without guilt.

He delights in cheerful givers—and also in cheerful receivers.

Fully Present with God

What is your current belief about wealth? What did you inherit, and what is God inviting you to rewrite?

Write the messages you absorbed growing up: *Money is evil. We never have enough. Rich people are greedy.* Then ask: What does God say?

_____

_____

_____

_____

_____

_____

_____

_____

_____

_____

_____

_____

_____

_____

_____

_____

_____

_____

_____

_____

_____

_____

_____

_____

Time: A Gift, Not a god

Time expands when we are with God. It was never meant to be a tyrant over us, but a beautiful gift created for our flourishing. Do you think Adam and Eve ever worried about running out of time in Eden?

Did they watch the sun anxiously, afraid the day was slipping away?

Or did they simply walk with God in the cool of the day, unhurried, at ease, knowing time was spacious and abundant?

In the Garden, time was fluid. The sun marked day, the moon marked night, but there was no panic in the passing hours—only presence. Time wasn't a master to serve, but a rhythm to enjoy.

Many of us today live as though time is our judge. We serve the clock like it's a god.

We measure our worth by our productivity.

We cram our calendars so full that peace feels like a luxury.

In that place, our bodies suffer. Anxiety rises. Our hearts race. Stress steals our breath.

When we honor time as a gift—when we slow down, notice, breathe—we begin to experience time differently.

Peace settles in. Our bodies soften. We taste ease instead of pressure, presence instead of panic.

Here's the mystery: the way we honor time now is a glimpse of eternity.

In heaven, time is not measured but overflowing.

There are no deadlines, no rushing, no fear of loss. Only an eternal "now" of joy, love, and communion with God.

Every time you choose to step out of urgency and into presence, you're practicing eternity.

You're aligning your body and spirit with the timelessness of heaven—a space where love expands, joy deepens, and peace is never interrupted.

Time is not your enemy. It is not "Father Time" ruling with a stern hand.

It is a gift from your Heavenly Father—one that expands in His presence, one that bends to bless you rather than break you.

Fully Present with God

Are you serving time, or stewarding it? What would it look like to trust God's rhythm instead of racing the clock?

Write how your body feels under time pressure—and how it feels when time flows with God's pace.

_____

_____

_____

_____

_____

_____

_____

_____

_____

_____

_____

_____

_____

_____

_____

_____

_____

_____

_____

_____

_____

_____

Grief: The Sacred Ache

Grief isn't something we just feel in our hearts—it shows up in our bodies.

Tightness in the chest. A heavy ache in the stomach. Fatigue that makes even the simplest tasks feel impossible.

Sometimes it's the lump in your throat that won't go away, or the way your body feels like it's carrying an invisible weight.

Our bodies are sacred spaces that tell the truth.

When grief rises, it isn't betrayal—it's your body showing you what needs to be honored.

Too often, we try to "fix" grief or rush past it. We medicate it with distraction, or bury it under busyness.

Grief isn't a problem to solve. It's an experience to be felt.

Jesus shows us this. Standing before Lazarus' tomb, knowing He was about to call His friend out of death and into life, He still wept.

The Son of God—the One who holds resurrection in His hands—allowed Himself to feel the full depth of grief.

Why? Because grief is love's echo. It's proof that what was lost mattered.

Grief is not weakness. Grief is holy. It carves out space for healing. It softens the soil of our hearts so that love can be planted again.

In the garden of your body, grief is not a weed to be pulled, but a season of rest and renewal.

Are you comfortable sitting with your own grief?

Can you resist the temptation to rush to "fix" it?

Can you sit with someone else's grief without trying to offer solutions?

Sometimes, presence is the most powerful gift. God's presence. Each other's presence. Simply being with. Being with is love.

Your body, as a holy garden, gives you feedback here, too.

The tears, the sighs, the deep breaths, even the trembling—these are not signs of failure.

They are signs of release. Signs that something sacred is moving through you.

Here's the breathtaking truth: God does not dismiss your tears. He treasures them. *"You have kept count of my tossings; put my tears in your bottle"* (Psalm 56:8).

Every tear you've ever cried is known, held, and honored by your Father.

The world often says strength is holding it all together, never breaking, never crying.

Heaven sees it differently.

In God's Kingdom, tears are powerful.

They water the soil of your soul. They are a prayer without words.

They testify to love that was real, connection that mattered, and hope that still lives.

So don't fear your tears. Don't silence your grief.

Let your tears flow like rain upon the garden of your body.

It is not weakness. It is holy. It is healing. It is beautiful and powerful.

Fully Present with God

What are you grieving right now?

Grief isn't limited to the death of someone we love. It can be the quiet ache of losing a friendship that once felt unshakable.

It can be the job you poured yourself into that no longer fits, or the dream that didn't unfold the way you hoped. It can be the loss of health, the changing of a season, or even the shedding of an identity—like stepping away from a religious framework that once gave you belonging but no longer feels like home.

Take a moment to pause and name it. What loss is your body carrying? What shift is your heart still tender from?

Can you let yourself feel it without rushing to move on, without labeling it "too small" or "not important enough"? Can you honor it as holy—trusting that God is with you even here, in the ache, tending the soil with His presence?

_____

_____

_____

_____

_____

_____

_____

_____

_____

_____

_____

_____

_____

Anger: Fire in the Right Hands

What is your relationship with anger?

We've been taught to fear it. To stuff it down. To judge it as weakness, or worse, as sin.

Yet anger is not foreign to God.

Scripture tells us of His righteous anger, and we see Jesus flipping tables in the temple—not to destroy, but to restore what was holy.

Anger is not the enemy. In its rightful place, it is a protector. A purifier. A force that rises up and says, *This is not good. This boundary has been crossed. This garden needs defending.*

When anger is not honored, it festers.

When we repress it, it doesn't disappear—it hides. It seeps into our bones as resentment, into our nervous system as anxiety, into our gut as toxicity.

Held too long, anger begins to poison us from the inside, twisting into bitterness, rage, or shame.

Our bodies start to keep the score that they were never intended to keep: clenched jaws, tight chests, shallow breath, restless nights.

When anger is acknowledged—named without judgment—it flows like every other healthy process in the body.

Like waste leaving the system. Like sweat released after strain. Like tears watering the soil.

Anger can be holy when it is surrendered.

Not wielded like a sword to cut others down, but laid at the feet of God.

Father, I feel this fire. I trust You to tend it. I trust You to bring justice and healing in ways I cannot.

When we release anger in love, it doesn't destroy—it clarifies.

It shows us where our boundaries are meant to be restored. It points to where something precious needs protection. It teaches us where change must happen.

What if your anger isn't here to ruin your peace—but to call you back to it?

You are not evil for feeling anger. You are human. And God delights in your humanity.

He gave you a body that speaks in many languages—joy, grief, and yes, even anger.

All of them are invitations to His presence.

The question is not, *Do you feel anger?* but *What will you do with it?*

Will you stuff it down until it poisons you? Or will you name it, honor it, and hand it back to the One whose love burns brighter than any fire in your chest?

Fully Present with God

Where do you feel anger lingering in your life? Is there something God is asking you to release—not out of denial, but as a form of trust?

Name it. Write what it feels like in your body. Then imagine placing it in God's hands.

_____

_____

_____

_____

_____

_____

_____

_____

_____

_____

_____

_____

_____

_____

_____

_____

_____

_____

_____

_____

_____

_____

Closing Blessing

May you tend to the hidden systems of your garden with love,
tenderness, and truth.
May your sexual wellness be sacred.
May your provision and finances flow.
May time be stewarded, not feared.
May your grief be honored.
May your anger be released in love.

And may you remember: nothing is off-limits to God.
Nothing is too messy for love.
He walks every inch of your garden. And He calls it good.

Amen.

HOW DOES REST LOOK IN YOUR GARDEN?

R est is not a reward. It is a rhythm. It is not the pause after the creating—it is part of the creation. It is not an interruption to your productivity. It is the very ground from which true fruitfulness grows.

Rest is the hardest part for many of us.

Let's begin where we always begin: with the truth.

How do you feel about rest?

Your Relationship with Rest

If you're like me, you may have grown up with a mindset that glorified exhaustion.

"You can sleep when you die," they said.

So I tried. And I almost didn't make it out alive.

To rest felt like defeat. Like weakness. Like failure.

Or maybe you're like my daughter, who as a toddler hated going to sleep. There was too much life to live. Too many things happening. The world felt full of possibility, and rest felt like missing out.

Do you feel like you're missing out when you rest? Like someone else might be winning while you're sleeping?

Let's shift that lens.

If you believe God is a loving Father—then rest is not the time when something is stolen from you.

It is a gift He is trying to give.

A gift you were never meant to earn.

The enemy wants to keep you pushing, demanding, overworking. Scarcity-driven. Proving your worth through action.

God already knows your worth. And He wants to remind you— through stillness.

Even God rests. On the seventh day, He paused.

Jesus rested. He retreated. He slept through storms. He pulled away from crowds.

So I ask you: how does rest look in your garden?

Fully Present with God

How do you currently feel when you rest? What emotions arise? Guilt? Fear? Peace? What might God want to speak into that space?

Write the first feelings that surface when you try to rest. Then ask: What would God say about this?

_____

_____

_____

_____

_____

_____

_____

_____

_____

_____

_____

_____

_____

_____

_____

_____

_____

_____

_____

_____

_____

What Is Rest, Really?

Rest is more than sleep. It is:

- Inner stillness
- Cellular repair
- Mental spaciousness
- Emotional permission
- Spiritual realignment

Rest is not "doing nothing". It is doing what heals.

It is laying down the need to prove. It is stepping away from the noise to return to your name.

Rest is not a weakness. It is warfare against scarcity.

It says: *I trust God more than my effort.*

Fully Present with God

Where have you equated rest with laziness? How might God be redefining that for you?

Be honest about the cultural or family beliefs you inherited about rest. What if rest is not weakness, but worship?

_____

_____

_____

_____

_____

_____

_____

_____

_____

_____

_____

_____

_____

_____

_____

_____

_____

_____

_____

Do You Trust What Happens When You Let Go?

Rest is trust in motion.
To rest is to release your grip.

To say: *God, I believe the world will keep turning even if I don't turn with it for a while.*

This was not easy for me.

I believed that if I wasn't constantly working, things would fall apart. People wouldn't love me. Things wouldn't get done right.

Beneath all of that? A lie.

The lie that I had to be God. That I had to be the center. That I had to hold everything together.

Now, with humility and love, I see it clearly: I'm not God. I don't need to be.

God invites me into rest not because I'm weak, but because I'm loved. His grace works best when I stop trying to do it all myself.

How Often Do You Rest?

Our culture counts everything: sleep cycles, rest days, hours clocked. God doesn't count like we do. He counts in wholeness, not in hours.

Rest doesn't have to be scheduled. It can be a moment. A breath. A surrender. A pause in the middle of a busy day.

The best rest I've ever received came when I stopped trying to control it.

There was a moment I was sitting in a chaotic airport in one of the most energetically tense cities I've ever experienced. I hadn't slept much. But I paused. I breathed. I sank into my body. And it felt like I had taken a three-hour nap.

Rest is not just sleep. It is restoration. And your body knows how to find it—if you listen.

Fully Present with God

What does restorative rest look like to your body today? Can you give yourself that gift without guilt?

Write one practical act of rest—a nap, silence, a walk, or time away from screens.

_____

_____

_____

_____

_____

_____

_____

_____

_____

_____

_____

_____

_____

_____

_____

_____

_____

_____

_____

_____

_____

The Places You Rest

Where is your restful place?

In bed? On a beach? In a hammock? In nature? At the feet of Jesus?

Where does your spirit exhale?

I'm partial to sand and waves. I've also found rest in unexpected places. I've rested in my car. In an airport terminal. On a park bench. Rest isn't always about where—it's about how.

Peter rested in prison. Jesus slept in a storm.

Rest transcends circumstance when it's rooted in trust.

You can cultivate rest anywhere. Because rest isn't a place you go. It's a posture you return to.

The Physiology of Rest

Rest is not just a concept—it's a physical necessity.

- Lowers cortisol (stress hormone)
- Regulates blood pressure
- Balances blood sugar
- Boosts immune response
- Promotes digestion and detoxification
- Supports hormone balance
- Aids in memory and learning

When we rest, our bodies shift from fight-or-flight (sympathetic nervous system) to rest-and-digest (parasympathetic nervous system).

Our bodies were made to cycle between work and recovery. Burnout is not spiritual. Burnout is a signal.

God never asked you to die on every hill. Jesus already did that.

Fully Present with God

How is your body currently asking for rest?

Notice the signals—fatigue, irritability, aches. Your body is speaking. Write what it's asking for.

_____

_____

_____

_____

_____

_____

_____

_____

_____

_____

_____

_____

_____

_____

_____

_____

_____

_____

_____

_____

_____

_____

_____

Rest as a Boundary

To rest in a culture of constant striving is an act of holy defiance.

To choose margin over overload. To say *no* when the world demands *yes.* To remember that your worth is not tied to your work.

This is revolutionary.

This is worship.

Even Jesus withdrew. Even He said, "Come away with Me and rest."

Rest is not stepping away from purpose. It is stepping into sustainability.

Rest is saying:

- I am not my productivity
- I am not my paycheck
- I am not my performance
- I am beloved, even in stillness

Fully Present with God

What systems in your life resist rest? What boundaries might God be inviting you to set?

Is it work? Family expectations? Social media? Write the pressures that resist rest and what boundary could create space.

_____

_____

_____

_____

_____

_____

_____

_____

_____

_____

_____

_____

_____

_____

_____

_____

_____

_____

_____

_____

_____

_____

_____

Sacred Rhythms: Reclaiming Sabbath

Sabbath is not a rule. It's a rhythm.

It is not about legalism. It's about liberation.

Sabbath was made for man, not the other way around.

Sabbath says:

- I am not a slave to time.
- I don't need to earn love.
- I can stop because He never does.

Imagine one day a week where:

- Your phone is silent
- Your meals are slow
- Your spirit breathes

It doesn't have to be Sunday. It doesn't have to be one day. It just gets to be sacred.

Sabbath is how we remember Eden. And how we rehearse heaven.

Letting Go to Lay Down

We cannot rest when we are gripping.

To lay down means:

- Letting go of control
- Loosening our need to fix
- Releasing our timeline

Rest often requires trust. That the world will keep spinning. That God will keep providing. That you don't have to be everything to everyone.

That He is God, and you are not.

Rest in the Body of Christ

Communal rest is just as holy as personal rest.

Imagine:

- Families choosing rest over performance
- Churches honoring pace over pressure or performance
- Leaders modeling sabbath, not burnout

You resting gives others permission to do the same.

You being gentle with yourself teaches others how to tend to themselves, too.

What if your garden could be a resting place for someone else?

How Will You Welcome Rest Today?

Can you allow yourself a holy pause?

Maybe that means stepping away from your desk.

Maybe it means saying no to one more task.

Maybe it means taking a walk. Or breathing slowly. Or soaking in stillness without needing to accomplish anything.

Rest is not a luxury. It is a necessity. It is a blessing.

And in your garden, it is the very soil that allows fruit to grow.

Closing Blessing

May you lay down the heavy yoke of proving.
May you sink deep into the soil of grace.
May rest find you not as a reward, but as a right.

May your nights be full of peace.
May your days hold moments of stillness.
May your garden be watered with rest.
May your spirit be unburdened from endless striving.
May your mind find stillness.
May your body find release.

May you sleep deeply and wake gently.
May you walk slowly and breathe fully.
And may you know—deep in your bones—that you are held, loved, and safe.
Even when you rest.
Especially when you rest.

Amen.

Part II

PHYSIOLOGY OF HEAVEN

Chapter 7

THE PHYSIOLOGY
OF LOVE

L ove is not just an idea. It is a physiological experience. It isn't just a feeling we talk about in church or read about in Scripture. Love is a force that moves through the body, shapes our breath, calms our systems, heals our wounds, and unlocks the deepest places of our being.

Love is not just a concept. It is a current. It moves through our thoughts, our organs, our cells. Love is the language of God. And our bodies were designed to speak it fluently.

Before we ever understand theology, before we can speak a word—we feel love. Or the absence of it. Our first breath and our last sigh both long to be cradled in it.

What does love do to your body? What happens physiologically when you live from the truth: *I am loved?*

The Foundation: You Are Loved

God is love. Not just loving. But the source of it.

When you experience true love—from God, from others, or from within yourself—your body reacts in real, measurable ways. You breathe deeper. Your muscles soften. Your immune system strengthens. Your nervous system begins to unwind.

Love tells your body, *"You are safe now."*

My experience of the Lord—above all else—is love. Everything flows from that truth. Faith and hope mean little without love as the soil they grow in. Scripture says so. And my body confirms it.

The Infinite Power of Love in the Body

So what happens to our body when we are loved unconditionally? What happens when we believe in that love?

When I feel the love of God—truly feel it—something changes in me. It's not just emotional. It's biological. My breath slows. My shoulders release. My mind clears. My immune system strengthens. My muscles stop bracing.

Love restores. It is the ultimate nervous system regulator. It is the great hormonal balancer. It is the original medicine.

This isn't only about receiving love from God. It's also about:

- The love we receive from others
- The love we give to others
- The love we receive from ourselves
- The love we give to ourselves

All of it matters. All of it shapes us.

Love and Fear: Two Different Languages

Love and fear are two languages—and our bodies hear both frequently.

Love is the language of God. Fear is the language of the enemy. Love expands. Fear contracts. Love invites. Fear isolates. Love softens the body. Fear stiffens it.

Sometimes we've confused them.

In Scripture, we're told to "fear the Lord." The word used often translates more accurately as "revere." Stand in awe. Be overcome with love, not afraid of punishment.

God has had to tell humanity over and over again: *Do not be afraid.* When we're in His presence, we don't need to flinch. We don't need to shrink. We don't need to hide. His perfect love casts out fear—not by force, but by healing.

The Hormonal Shift: Oxytocin and Beyond

Oxytocin is often called the "love hormone." It's released when we hug, laugh, pray, meditate, connect, or simply feel safe. It promotes bonding. It reduces stress. It helps the body heal.

Let's talk about this differently. Let's not turn love into a chemical transaction. Let's remember that our chemistry reflects our Creator. That oxytocin and cortisol, dopamine and serotonin—these are systems God designed to show us when we are aligned with His heart.

When we feel loved—by God, by others, or by ourselves—our body returns to its natural, divine rhythm. We were made to live in love. And the body reveals it.

Love from God: Safety at the Cellular Level

What happens in your body when you believe—truly believe—that God loves you?

Not tolerates you. Not loves the future version of you. But delights in you, right now.

That belief is grounding. It slows your heart rate. It centers your breathing. It releases a cascade of safety chemicals that tell your body: *I don't have to brace for impact.*

God's love is not earned. It is embedded. Receiving it doesn't make you weak. It makes you whole.

Spiritual connection through prayer, worship, and intimacy with the Lord slows our breath, reduces inflammation, eases the nervous system, and brings the brain into coherence.

This isn't religious hype. It's embodied reality.

When I meditate on God's love for me—when I imagine Him smiling at me—my body relaxes. My heart opens. My immune system strengthens. My perspective softens.

Love heals us from the inside out.

Love from Others: The Gift of Human Connection

We are wired for connection. From the moment we are born, our bodies seek comfort in the faces of others. We were never meant to do life alone.

When we experience love through relationships—friendship, family, romance, or community—our entire physiology shifts.

Loving relationships reduce blood pressure. They increase lifespan. They help us heal from injury and illness faster. They remind us we are not alone.

Whether it's the touch of a friend, the encouragement of a spouse, or the presence of a parent—love from others nourishes our garden.

Even brief moments of connection—a kind word, eye contact, shared laughter—can shift our entire physiology:

- Your blood pressure lowers
- Your digestion improves
- Your brain fog clears
- Your muscles release tension

We were made for connection. And love expressed through others reminds us: we are not alone.

Love for Others: The Overflow

Giving love is just as healing as receiving it.

Acts of service, expressions of affection, praying for others—these create meaning in the body. The more love you give, the more your internal systems harmonize.

You weren't made to be a reservoir. You were made to be a river. And as you pour out, you are refilled.

Jesus said, *"Love one another as I have loved you."* He knew this wasn't just spiritual instruction—but physiological wisdom.

Love protects your heart. Literally.

Self-Love: The Ground We Walk On

Self-love is not selfish. It is foundational. You cannot pour from an empty cup.

More importantly—you don't need to earn your own kindness. You don't have to put yourself last, or finish everything on your list before you care for your body and soul.

Love doesn't demand that you prove yourself first; it simply invites you to receive.

Loving yourself means:

- Speaking kindly to your body
- Listening to your needs
- Honoring your boundaries
- Choosing rest when needed
- Celebrating your growth

You cannot tend a garden you hate.

Self-love is sacred stewardship.

When you speak kindly to yourself, when you listen to your body, when you rest without guilt—your whole system responds:

- Your skin glows
- Your digestion improves
- Your energy stabilizes
- Your immune response strengthens

Shame shuts down healing. Love opens the gates. Self-love is not a luxury. It is a life source.

It starts in small ways:

- A deep breath
- A nourishing meal
- Saying "no" without apology
- Saying "yes" to what restores

It means seeing yourself the way God sees you.

When I began to love myself not from ego but from grace, my entire health shifted. My muscles stopped being on alert. My sleep improved. My digestion calmed. My thoughts softened.

The body knows when it is loved.

Love and Healing: A Whole-Body Response

Love reduces cortisol, the stress hormone. Love boosts immunity. Love enhances muscle recovery. Love supports cardiovascular health. Love increases resilience. Love invites flow.

When we live in love, we breathe differently. We move differently. We digest differently. We think differently. We relate differently.

Love is not a feeling. It is a function. It is a flow. It is a force of divine healing. And it is available now. Not when you earn it. Not when you fix everything. Now.

Fully Present with God

Take these prompts slowly, as if they are a conversation between you, your body, and God. Breathe deeply. Let yourself soften into the truth that you are already loved—fully, freely, and without condition.

When was the last time you truly felt loved by God?
Close your eyes and bring that moment to mind.

Was it during prayer, a quiet walk, a surprising provision, or a whisper in your spirit?

Where did you feel it in your body? A warmth in your chest, a loosening of your shoulders, a deep sigh of relief?

Write it down, not just as a memory, but as a reminder that His love is alive in you right now.

What does self-love look like in your daily practice?
Think small, gentle acts. Is it choosing nourishing food, giving yourself permission to rest, or speaking kindly to yourself when you make a mistake?

Write down what self-love currently looks like—and also what you long for it to be. What one practice could you add tomorrow as a simple act of love toward yourself?

How does love from others affect your physical health?
Notice how your body responds when you receive love freely— whether through a smile, a hug, words of affirmation, or simply someone's presence.

Do you breathe easier? Sleep better? Feel less tension?

Write about how love from others restores you. And also, how does the absence of love or conditional love weigh on your body? Naming this is part of healing.

What would it look like to live in the physiology of love? Imagine your body not just surviving, but literally flourishing because of love. Cells regenerating, your nervous system at peace, your heart radiant with joy.

Imagine love as the atmosphere you breathe in daily—shaping your choices, your posture, your relationships.

Write what it would mean for you to embody love in every part of your being.

_____

_____

_____

_____

_____

_____

_____

_____

_____

_____

_____

_____

_____

_____

_____

Fear: The Opposite Current

If love is the language of God, fear is the dialect of the enemy.

Fear constricts. Love expands. Fear floods the body with cortisol, spikes heart rate, narrows focus, wastes energy. It tells the body to brace, prepare, withdraw.

Perfect love casts out fear. Not through punishment. But through presence.

When we encounter fear, the invitation is not to suppress it—but to surround it in love.

God is not angry at your fear. He knows what you're up against. He meets you in it. He whispers: *You are still mine. You are still safe. You are still loved.*

Your body begins to believe again.

Fear is woven into the fabric of this world, Heaven has no fear or trace of the enemy's presence based on my experience.

God is not surprised when you experience fear again, trust that His love will cast it out.

One practice that helps me is a simple visualization I share with God: together, we take the fear, lie, or accusing thought that doesn't belong and hold it like a ball.

Then, I picture punting that ball far out of the stadium—out of my sight, out of my mind. As it leaves, space opens inside me.

Peace rushes in to remind me of the truth of who I am: beloved, safe, and free

Sometimes I'm punting all day, sometimes I don't remember punting once during the day.

All days are blessed, and I do notice when fatigue, stress, obligations pile up, I'm usually punting a lot more that day.

Love as Lifelong Nourishment

Love is not a one-time experience. It is daily bread. Every moment you align with love, you feed your body truth. Every time you let yourself be held by God's affection, you align your biology with heaven.

Love heals wounds that medicine can't reach. Love builds resilience where trauma once reigned. Love re-patterns the body to feel safe, connected, and whole.

Your body was made for love. Let it return.

Closing Blessing

May love flow through every cell in your body.
May your muscles soften, your breath deepen, and your heart feel safe.
May you know the Father's delight. May you feel the embrace of divine love.

May you give love freely. Receive love deeply. And return to love whenever you forget.
Love is your beginning. Love is your design. Love is your healing.

And may your whole garden blossom under love's endless light.

Amen.

Chapter 2

THE PHYSIOLOGY OF THE MIRACULOUS

W hat is the miraculous? And maybe more importantly—where did your definition come from?

Did your belief in miracles come from religion? From science? From family? From a lack of evidence? From a lifetime of hoping for a miracle and not seeing it?

Or maybe from experiencing a miracle you still don't have words for.

We all carry stories and expectations about what miracles are.

So often, we don't realize we've slipped into a limited, logical belief system until something comes along that shatters it—an experience that cracks open our assumptions and awakens us to a reality greater than we imagined. Suddenly, what once felt impossible becomes possible.

This chapter is an invitation to open yourself again—to imagine again. To let your body, even more than your thoughts, become the living garden where the miraculous takes root and blooms daily. Not as a rare interruption, but as your new normal—a reality you are free to choose and walk in.

What Is the Miraculous?

The miraculous, in my experience, is not just an event. It is a shift. A doorway. A divine intervention that leaves a physiological imprint.

The miraculous is anything that reveals God's hand clearly in our lives.

It can be:

- The sudden healing
- The impossible provision
- The divine timing
- The whisper that becomes a rescue
- The moment of clarity that wasn't there before

It can also be:

- The peace that passes understanding
- The breath that returns when panic tried to take it
- The love that softens a hardened heart

The miraculous is not always dramatic. Sometimes, it's quiet. And the body still knows.

What Does Healing Really Mean?

We often think healing is recovery from an injury or illness. Divine healing is something deeper. Healing is not just the absence of pain or symptoms. Healing is the restoration of wholeness.

It is continuous, infinite.

Healing is how our cells—and our whole body—return to their true nature after exposure to anything that causes harm.

It's the body remembering it was designed for life. It's the cells aligning with joy. It's the nervous system relaxing into peace.

True healing is miraculous—even when it unfolds slowly.

Even when it doesn't look like what we prayed for.

Is the Miraculous Possible in My Body?

We must first challenge what we've accepted.
As a person believes in their heart, so they become—body, mind, and spirit.
Have you accepted chronic pain as your forever story?
Have you accepted fatigue, tension, or imbalance as permanent guests?

I have. I've caught myself bracing my body in subtle ways—anticipating discomfort like it was my norm.

But what about the other stories we've been told to accept?

Have we quietly agreed that arthritis is just inevitable as we age?

Have we believed menopause must be miserable, full of suffering instead of wisdom and renewal?

Have we resigned ourselves to our genetics—heart disease, cancer, depression—as if family history must dictate our future?

Have you accepted that brain fog and memory loss are simply a normal part of getting older?

Have you accepted that your metabolism has to slow down, leaving you with no choice but to feel heavier and less alive in your body?

Have you accepted that stress, anxiety, or sleepless nights are just part of "modern life"?

I choose something different now.

What if we stopped accepting dysfunction as our design?

hat if the miraculous is available not just in emergencies, but in daily restoration?

The truth is: God created the body with astonishing adaptability. Regeneration. Neuroplasticity. Hormonal harmony. Cellular repair.

Science calls it resilience.

I call it a miracle in motion

The Physical Gifts of the Miraculous

When we open ourselves to the miraculous—when we allow faith, love, and God's presence to shape our daily lives—our bodies respond in ways that science is only beginning to glimpse.

The miraculous doesn't bypass the body. It works through it, often in ways measurable, tangible, and transformative.

Here's what belief in, or experience of, the miraculous can do for the body:

- **Extend life expectancy**
  People who live with faith, gratitude, and hope often live longer, healthier lives. Stress decreases, resilience increases, and the body thrives. Scripture calls it "life to the full."

  Faith has a way of literally adding years to our lives—not by fear-driven striving, but by living in trust and love.

- **Boost the immune system**
  When we live in peace instead of fear, our immune defenses rise. Prayer, meditation, and living in God's love shift our nervous system out of fight-or-flight and into rest-and-restore.

  The miraculous often looks like colds fading faster, chronic conditions lessening, inflammation reducing—all because the body is freed to do what God designed it to do.

- **Imprint on our memory**
  Miraculous experiences leave a lasting mark, not just on our spirit but in the brain itself.

  Memory circuits capture the moment of awe, wonder, or healing, reminding us of God's goodness even years later.

  They become anchors of faith—reminders that if He did it once, He can do it again.

- **Create new neural connections**
  Science calls it neuroplasticity. Faith calls it renewal.
  When we encounter God in love, the brain literally rewires.
  Pathways of fear can be replaced with pathways of peace.
  Trauma can be re-scripted.

  Joy can become our default setting instead of anxiety.

  This is the miraculous written in our neurons.

- **Accelerate physical healing**
  Broken bones mending faster than expected. Cancers
  shrinking. Chronic pain easing in ways doctors can't explain.

  These stories are more common than we realize. Sometimes
  it's instantaneous. Other times it unfolds gradually.

  They always it points to the truth: God designed the body
  with extraordinary capacity to heal—and He loves to breathe
  on that process.

- **Slow aging, increase vitality**
  The miraculous doesn't just heal—it rejuvenates.

  People who live immersed in God's presence often look and
  feel younger. Skin glows. Energy flows. Cells regenerate.

  Joy has a way of showing up on the face and in the body.

- **Expand physical capacity**
  There are moments when the miraculous gives strength
  beyond what the body "should" have—running farther,
  lifting more, enduring longer.

  Just as Elijah was strengthened to run miles ahead of Ahab's
  chariot (1 Kings 18:46), our bodies can be supernaturally
  sustained when filled with God's Spirit.

The question isn't whether miracles can happen. They do. The question
is: **Are you open to believe and receive them?**

What Is Possible for Your Body?

That's the question I want you to carry.

Not what have you been told. Not what's been diagnosed. Not what's in your family line.

What is possible if you believe God is infinitely good and for your infinite good?

What is possible if love really is the strongest force in the universe?

What is possible if your body was designed not just to survive—but to reflect heaven?

Fully Present with God

Take your time with these prompts. They are not a checklist but an invitation. Breathe. Pause. Let your heart rest open to the God who delights in bringing heaven into your body and your life.

Where in your body do you long to see the miraculous?

Is it in a place of pain, illness, or tension? Maybe in your mind where anxiety or heaviness lingers? Write it down honestly.

Hold it before God like an offering. Whisper, *"Father, this is where I long for You to move."* Ask Him to show you what's possible, and watch how His peace begins to meet you in that very place.

What have you accepted as permanent in your body or health?

Pause here. Many of us quietly resign ourselves to "that's just how it is"—aches with age, family history of disease, ongoing fatigue.

Write those beliefs down without judgment. Then ask: *What if these aren't permanent? What if God has something more?*

Have you ever experienced a moment that felt miraculous?

Maybe it was a sudden healing, a timely word, or a peace that came out of nowhere. Remember that moment.

Where did you feel it in your body? Did your shoulders relax, your breath deepen, your heart expand?

Write down the sensations so you can recall them when doubt creeps in.

What is possible if you believe God is infinitely good and for your infinite good?

Close your eyes and imagine what would shift if this truth anchored every part of your being.

How would you live differently if you truly trusted that God's goodness was not limited—but overflowing into every cell, every breath, every choice?

What is possible if your body was designed not just to survive—but to reflect heaven?

Your body is not an accident. It is sacred ground. Imagine your cells shimmering with vitality, your mind at rest, your spirit glowing with peace.

Write about what it would mean for you to live as a walking reflection of heaven's wholeness here on earth.

_____

_____

_____

_____

_____

_____

_____

_____

_____

_____

_____

_____

_____

_____

The Body's Response to Awe

Awe is the physiological cousin of the miraculous.

Awe:

- Slows our breath
- Lowers inflammation
- Increases vagal tone (a marker of nervous system health)
- Expands our perception of time
- Enhances empathy and compassion

When we witness the miraculous, awe floods the system. It grounds us. It opens us to more possibilities.

Faith and the Placebo Effect

Belief is powerful. The placebo effect is not fake healing. It's real healing triggered by expectation.

When the brain believes something good is happening, it releases endorphins, dopamine, and even activates immune cells.

Faith does something similar.
It opens the body to possibility. It breaks the loop of despair.
It tells your systems: hope is not dangerous. It is powerful.

Miracles and the Nervous System

Many who experience a miracle describe physical symptoms:

- Tingling in the spine or scalp
- Sudden tears or sobbing
- Goosebumps
- Heat or lightness in the body

These aren't just emotional reactions. They are physiological responses to a spiritual encounter.

When God touches earth, your body feels it.

Just as wind flows through your nervous system, the Spirit moves over and through you—gently caressing the earth within.

Healing and Wholeness

Some miracles are instant. Some are slow. Some are in the body. Some are in the soul. But all are rooted in one truth: God wants you whole, the truth of your being.

Miraculous healing happens when:

- Stress is replaced by peace
- Cells begin regenerating instead of breaking down
- Immune function heightens
- Blood pressure stabilizes

The body is reminded: healing is your default, not your exception.

You are wired for restoration.

Living Open to the Miraculous

Children believe in miracles easily.

Have you noticed how quickly their bodies heal? How effortlessly they bounce back?

They haven't yet been taught what's "impossible."
So what happens when we return to that posture—of wonder, of trust, of wide-open belief?

What begins to heal when we stop bracing and start believing again?

Living open to the miraculous looks like:

- Expecting beauty
- Asking boldly
- Listening gently
- Trusting your body to be a vessel for heaven

Fully Present with God

What beliefs about miracles would you like to release—or reclaim?

Take a quiet moment with your journal. Write down the stories, sayings, or experiences that may have shaped how you see miracles—"Miracles are rare," "God doesn't work like that anymore," or "Healing is for other people, not me."

Then ask yourself: *Do these beliefs align with the God of love, abundance, and restoration?* If not, release them. Cross them out. Tear the page if you need to.

Now consider the beliefs you'd like to reclaim. Maybe it's the childlike faith you once had. Maybe it's the testimony of a healing you've witnessed. Maybe it's the simple truth that "with God all things are possible." Write them down and let them take root.

What would it mean for you to live with an open heart to the miraculous today?

Close your eyes and imagine moving through today as if miracles were not the exception, but the norm.

What would shift in your body if you trusted healing was already flowing? How would you speak differently if you believed your words carried creative power? How would you love, forgive, or show up in your relationships if you expected God to move?

Write down one small, tangible way you can posture your heart toward the miraculous today—whether it's praying with expectancy, blessing your food as sacred nourishment, or simply pausing to breathe and whisper, *"I am walking in God's miracle now."*

_____

_____

_____

The Miraculous Within the Mundane

Your body performs miracles every day:

- Turning food into fuel
- Regenerating cells
- Healing wounds
- Interpreting light into vision
- Holding memory, music, and mystery in the same space

We tend to miss these daily wonders because they feel "normal."

The same God who parts seas also keeps your heart beating through the night. Let that sink in.

Closing Blessing

May your body be open to miracles.
May your cells remember their divine design.
May your mind expand to include what you once thought impossible.

May you release the need to control outcomes. And rest in the God who restores all things.

You are already walking in the miraculous.
May your garden bloom accordingly.

Amen.

Chapter 3

THE PHYSIOLOGY OF JOY AND TIME

J oy and time are lovers in the garden. They dance together. They bend toward the light. One softens the other. One gives space to the other.

I often visualize time as a majestic tree in my garden—rooted, abundant, playful. Like the tree in *The Giving Tree*, time itself rejoices in our joy. It bends its branches to meet us in the moment. It stretches itself when we're in presence. And like any loving parent, it delights in our childlike wonder.

Joy doesn't erase time. It transforms it. When we're in joy, time seems to slow—allowing us to savor. Or it speeds up—flying by in laughter and lightness.

The God who created time made it flexible, bendable, even expandable for joy.

Think of moments where time "slowed down" in wonder. Or "flew by" in delight. That was the physiology of joy and time merging in your body.

God, in His wisdom, gave us time not as a tyrant, but as a companion. And joy is how we sanctify it.

Come Share in Your Father's Joy

Scripture doesn't just say God *has* joy. It says He invites us to share in it. That's not duty. That's delight. That's inheritance.

For many of us, joy has been tangled up with guilt. We've been told faith is serious business, that God is stern, always watching for mistakes. Maybe you've inherited an image of Him as an angry, cranky old man—arms crossed, hurling lightning bolts, muttering about sin, demanding that you shape up. A God who keeps score. A God who yells, *"Get off my lawn!"*

No wonder joy feels suspicious in that worldview. No wonder laughter feels unsafe, as though God might be offended by our happiness.

That picture is not God. That's religion's distortion.

The real God—the God I met in **The River**—is joy itself.

His joy is the deep current that flows beneath all of heaven. It is the kind of joy that erases pain, the joy that makes sorrow temporary, the joy that is written into the fabric of creation.

He is the God who dances in delight. The God who sings over us with love. The Father who smiles when we create, when we rest, when we play.

He is not allergic to our happiness—He authored it.

When we wash off the false image of a grumpy, scowling God, we begin to breathe differently. We begin to live without the fear that joy will be "taken away" as punishment.

We begin to see joy as our natural state in Him, not something we must earn or feel guilty about.

This is freedom: to live in joy without shame, to know your Father's smile is real and it's directed at you.

Joy vs. Happiness

Some religious teachings split joy and happiness:

- Joy is spiritual, long-lasting, a gift from God.
- Happiness is shallow, temporary, tied to circumstances.

What if both are holy? What if happiness isn't the enemy of joy, but its spark?

What if every giggle, every sunset smile, every moment of awe is a seed of eternal joy?

God isn't threatened by our pleasure. He created our bodies to feel it.

Whether you call it joy, delight, play, or pleasure—it all brings you closer to the heart of God.

Joy in the Body: A Divine Design

Joy doesn't just happen *to* us—it happens *in* us. It's not an accessory to life; it's a divine force woven into our very biology. When we live in joy, our bodies respond as if heaven itself is singing through our cells.

Here's what science shows—and Scripture confirms:

- **Enhances immune response:** Joy strengthens your defenses. Studies show that positive emotional states increase the production of antibodies and bolster your body's ability to fight illness. Joy makes your immune system alert and ready.
- **Calms the nervous system:** Joy is like still waters for your nerves. It lowers stress hormones like cortisol and shifts your body into "rest and restore" mode. Your heart rate slows. Your breath deepens. Your body says, *I am safe.*
- **Releases tension and reduces pain:** Joy isn't naïve—it doesn't pretend pain doesn't exist. But it changes the way pain is processed in the brain and body. Laughter literally triggers the release of endorphins, easing discomfort and loosening the grip of chronic tension.

- **Adds years to life—and life to years:** Research confirms what Proverbs 17:22 said all along: *"A joyful heart is good medicine."* Joy doesn't just extend your lifespan; it improves the quality of those years. It infuses ordinary days with vibrancy, clarity, and hope.

But beyond the science, joy is holy. It's the Spirit dancing through your cells, declaring, *"You are alive, you are loved, you are mine."* It's heaven manifesting in your nervous system, your breath, your bloodstream.

Joy is not frivolous. It is foundational. It's not an escape from reality—it's an infusion of God's reality into ours.

So when joy rises in you, whether through laughter, gratitude, music, or a quiet sunrise, don't dismiss it. Bless it. Lean into it. Receive it as medicine, miracle, and sacred connection with your Creator.

Determination vs. Joyful Flow

We've been taught to hustle. To grind. To prove. The world says validation comes after exhaustion, after sacrifice, after you've "earned it."

God tells a different story. Before Jesus ever preached a sermon, healed the sick, or carried the cross, the Father spoke over Him: *"This is my Son, in whom I am well pleased."* (Matthew 3:17)

No miracles yet. No ministry launched. No résumé of accomplishments. Just sonship. Just love.

That is the soil we're invited to live from—joyful identity, not anxious striving.

Joy isn't the *reward* for performance. Joy is the *starting place of creation.*

When you create from joy, you can pause when your body asks for rest instead of pushing past your limits. You can trust God's rhythm instead of wearing yourself out with your own.

Because here's the truth: **it isn't really victory if it costs you your well-being.**

The promotion, the bank account, the book, the ministry, the "success"—if it comes attached with burnout, sickness, or fractured relationships, it's not the kind of blessing God gives.

"The blessing of the Lord makes one rich, and He adds no sorrow with it."
— Proverbs 10:22 (NKJV)

Or as the NIV says: *"The blessing of the Lord brings wealth, without painful toil for it."*

God's blessing doesn't carry hidden costs. It doesn't require you to sacrifice your peace, your health, or your joy to "keep it." That's the counterfeit version the world sells.

The Kingdom way is different.

It's flow, not force.

Grace, not grind.

Abundance, not anxiety.

When joy sets the boundary for your efforts, creativity comes more naturally. Ideas rise without pressure. Energy flows without depletion. The work of your hands multiplies without destroying the vessel of your body.

The Father's invitation is simple: Trust His abundance. Let joy be your compass. Watch how life unfolds when you choose His flow over the world's hustle.

The Pace of Joy

Joy doesn't rush.

It walks slowly through the garden.

It notices. It lingers. It smiles. It receives.

You don't rush through a sunrise—you soak in its light.

You don't gulp down a feast of love—you savor it.

Jesus Himself walked everywhere. He didn't sprint from miracle to miracle. He lingered at tables, told stories that unfolded slowly, stopped in the middle of a crowd to touch the overlooked. He napped in storms. He reclined with friends. He moved at the pace of eternity, not the pressure of urgency.

That's what joy looks like—unhurried, unforced, unafraid of missing out.

And when we match that pace, our bodies begin to remember how they were designed to live:

- **Your metabolism balances**—because stress isn't driving your digestion.
- **Your hormones regulate**—because your body finally believes it's safe.
- **Your gut flora stabilizes**—because you're nourishing instead of depleting yourself.
- **Your aging process slows**—because peace restores cells faster than striving ever could.

Victory is already ours. The cross secured it. Heaven has no stopwatch ticking against you. So what's the hurry?

The rush to prove, to keep up, to not fall behind—that doesn't come from God. It comes from fear. Fear says, "If I don't hurry, I'll miss my chance."

Joy says, "I can't miss what the Father has already given me."

Moving at the pace of joy doesn't mean laziness. It means alignment. It means trusting that the One who authored your story has already written the victory into every chapter.

When you live like that, your body can exhale. Your nervous system loosens its grip. Your whole being begins to flow with divine ease.

The invitation is simple: **Lay down the stopwatch. Pick up the sunrise. Let your life move at the pace of joy.**

Joy in Action: Matching Passion to Purpose

Here's a practical invitation, one that might surprise you with how much it reveals:

1. **Write down 50 things that bring you joy.** Don't edit. Don't judge. Let yourself list everything—from small delights like fresh-cut flowers, beach walks, or a favorite meal, to big dreams like traveling the world, painting, mentoring, or building community. Think of the things that light you up, that give you energy rather than drain it.
2. **Write down 50 things that generate income—or could grow into a career.** This could include your current work, skills you've developed, side hustles, or even ideas you've never acted on but know could bless others. Get creative: writing, coaching, designing, organizing, teaching, building, healing— what do you know how to do, or what would you love to learn?
3. **Now, compare the lists. Look for the overlaps.** Where do joy and provision intersect? Where do your delights already contain seeds of purpose and possibility?

This isn't just a career exercise. It's a spiritual practice. It's a way of aligning your God-given joy with your God-given calling.

Think about it—what if the very things that make you come alive are also the things that can sustain you? What if joy isn't separate from provision but the doorway to it?

When you notice the commonalities, you begin to see how joy creates careers, income, and opportunities—not just for survival, but for flourishing. For example:

- Love teaching children? That joy could expand into tutoring, homeschooling support, or children's books.

177

- Love cooking? That joy could spark a catering business, a food blog, or community dinners that draw people to God's table.
- Love connecting with people? That joy could grow into coaching, counseling, sales, or ministry.

Our enjoyment and God's glory are not opposites. They are synonymous.

When you delight in what He's placed in you, you reflect His image. Your joy is worship. Your flourishing is testimony.

And when you create from joy instead of striving, your body notices. Fatigue lessens. Clarity sharpens. Productivity flows like water instead of being wrung out of stone. This isn't hustle—it's holy alignment.

Remember: *God loves a cheerful giver—not just of money, but of time, attention, and creativity.* When you give from joy, the gift multiplies, blessing both you and the world around you.

So grab your journal, take your time, and really engage with this practice.

Let yourself dream. Let yourself imagine. You may just find that joy has already been preparing the blueprint for your next chapter of abundance.

Joy vs. World-Weariness

Let's be real. We live in a time of nonstop information. News cycles. Notifications. Stories of suffering. Injustice. Despair.

We weren't meant to carry the weight of the entire world's pain at every moment.

Connection without proximity can flood our nervous system.

So what do we do?

We grieve with the grieving. We fight injustice as God leads. But we also protect our joy.

You are allowed to:

- Turn off the news
- Say no to urgency
- Laugh even when the world is aching

God is not calling you to be the Savior. He already sent one.

Joy is not betrayal. Joy is alignment.

What Joy Looks Like in the Body

Think about the last time you laughed so hard you couldn't breathe—the kind of laughter that leaves your cheeks sore and your belly aching in the best way. What happened afterward?

- Your **skin glowed** as blood flow increased to the surface, carrying oxygen and nutrients.
- Your **shoulders softened**, dropping the weight of stress you didn't even realize you were holding.
- Your **eyes sparkled** with life, connection, and light.

Joy doesn't just feel good—it transforms the very landscape of your body.

Here's what science shows is happening:

- **Cells regenerate more efficiently**: laughter releases growth hormones that stimulate repair and renewal.
- **Digestion improves**: joy activates the parasympathetic nervous system (rest and digest mode), easing bloating and gut discomfort.
- **Blood sugar stabilizes**: stress hormones like cortisol drop, allowing insulin to work more effectively.
- **Fat storage decreases**: when stress goes down, your body no longer hoards energy in survival mode.
- **Inflammation lowers**: joy reduces inflammatory markers, supporting long-term health.
- **Pain sensitivity decreases**: laughter triggers endorphins, the body's natural pain relievers.

Beyond the science, joy changes how we carry ourselves:

- You breathe more deeply.
- You stand taller.
- You connect more easily with others.
- You return to your natural rhythm of rest, flow, and presence.

Joy puts your body in the healing zone. It shifts you from defense into delight. From survival into renewal.

Laughter, delight, play—these are not distractions from your healing journey. They *are* the healing. They are medicine written into your design by the Creator who smiles when you smile.

Joy is not optional for your health. **Joy *is* health.**

Fully Present with God

Joy is not something we have to chase—it's a gift woven into the fabric of who we are. These prompts are an invitation to pause, notice, and allow joy to flow again in your body and your sense of time.

What does joy mean to you right now?

Does joy look like laughter? Peace? A deep exhale? Or simply the absence of striving? Write what joy feels like for you in this season—not what you think it *should* be, but how it actually shows up.

What brings you joy—big or small?

A warm meal, sunshine on your skin, a child's smile, the sound of waves. Let your body remember these moments and notice how it responds. Do your shoulders drop? Does your chest feel lighter?

Have you allowed yourself to experience joy lately?

Sometimes we withhold joy until the "to-do list" is finished. What would it look like to give yourself permission to enjoy—even in the middle of the unfinished?

What beliefs about joy and time would you like to release?

Have you believed there isn't "enough time" for joy? Or that joy must be earned? Write the old beliefs—and then write a new truth: *Joy is available to me now, in this moment.*

_____

_____

_____

_____

_____

_____

_____

Joy and Eternity

God operates from joy. He didn't create the cosmos with a scowl on His face or exhaustion in His hands—He spoke galaxies into being with laughter, with song, with delight. Creation itself is the overflow of divine joy.

Scripture tells us that *in His presence is fullness of joy* (Psalm 16:11). Joy is not just a feeling—it is the atmosphere of heaven. It's the very soundtrack of eternity. Angels don't groan in duty; they sing in delight. The Kingdom of Heaven is not built on fear or striving but on righteousness, peace, **and joy in the Holy Spirit** (Romans 14:17).

What if we stopped treating joy as something reserved for "someday" and began practicing it *now*?

- What if laughter became our prophecy—a way of announcing that sorrow will not have the final word?
- What if delight became our declaration—that Heaven's abundance is already breaking into Earth?
- What if every time we chose joy, we were training our bodies for eternity?

Your laughter is not trivial—it echoes Heaven.

Your delight is not selfish—it is sacred participation in the divine rhythm of creation.

Each time you choose joy, your body learns eternity. Your cells carry light. Your nervous system rewires toward peace. Your garden grows lush with heaven's vibrancy.

We don't have to wait to die to live in heaven's joy. We can begin today—singing, laughing, dancing, savoring beauty. Every act of joy is a foretaste of eternity.

Joy is heaven now. Joy is eternity practiced today.

Closing Blessing

May joy be your rhythm.
May time bend like branches to hold your delight.
May your body be lit from within.
May your moments be saturated with joy.
May your time become a companion, not a taskmaster.
May you giggle freely.
May you rest easily.
May you dance without shame.
May your bones loosen in laughter.
May your eyes crinkle in delight.
May you feast on goodness without guilt.
May you breathe joy like oxygen.

God shares His joy with you. You are not a burden to Him. You are His beloved child. And your joy is holy.

Amen.

Chapter 4

THE PHYSIOLOGY
OF FREEDOM

In the very first breath of creation, God gives humanity choice. "Of every tree of the garden you may freely eat..."

Including the tree of the knowledge of good and evil. He placed freedom right in the center of the story.

Not tucked away in rules.

Not buried in systems.

Not earned through performance.

Freedom was given. Freely.

Just like in Eden, God still honors our choice—every single day. He never forces. He invites. He doesn't demand. He delights.

Freedom isn't just a political concept or a spiritual metaphor. It is a physiological necessity.

When your body feels free, it heals.

When your body feels trapped, it braces, hardens, and disconnects from flow.

We were made in the image of a God who gives choice. Not control.

The very first moment in the garden of Eden centers around freedom.

185

The Tree of Knowledge—unrestricted access to it. No gates. No forcefields. No Tree in a space where humanity could never reach.

Trust from the Creator of all.

Because love requires freedom. And the body does too.

What Does Freedom Feel Like in the Body?

It's easy to talk about freedom as a lofty, spiritual idea. But true freedom—*God's freedom*—is not just a concept. It lands in your body. It has texture. It has breath. It feels like release.

Freedom is not just something you believe. It's something you experience in your nervous system, your muscles, your breath, your cells.

- It's the release of clenched muscles that have carried too much for too long.
- It's the expansion of your lungs as breath flows fully and freely, no longer shallow or restricted.
- It's the slowing of your heartbeat when fear and striving are replaced with trust and presence.
- It's the quieting of racing thoughts—the stillness that comes when shame no longer narrates your story.
- It's the exhale after what feels like a lifetime of holding your breath, finally realizing: *I am safe. I am held. I am free.*

Freedom changes your biology. Stress hormones lower. Blood pressure balances. Immune systems strengthen. Your body stops bracing for battle and begins to heal.

Freedom looks like shoulders dropping, jaws unclenching, and a spine no longer curved in defeat but lifted in dignity. It feels like laughter rising unforced, like tears flowing without fear, like dancing without apology.

This is the kind of freedom God offers: not abstract, not theoretical, but embodied. A freedom that doesn't just stay in your mind but radiates into your cells. A freedom that isn't earned through striving but gifted through love.

Freedom is God's design—and when you feel it in your body, you begin to live Eden here and now.

Bondage, Control, and the Stress Response

When we live in limitation—whether financial, emotional, spiritual, relational, or systemic—our bodies keep score. Even if our mind tries to rationalize or push it down, our nervous system doesn't lie. It knows when we're in bondage.

Bondage feels like **tightness**—in your chest, your jaw, your gut. It feels like your breath never makes it all the way down, like you're only surviving on half an inhale. It feels like tossing in bed at night, unable to find rest because your body is on guard.

This is the stress response:

- **Fight** — snapping in anger, pushing harder, your body buzzing with adrenaline.
- **Flight** — restless, never settled, always busy, unable to sit still without guilt.
- **Freeze** — paralyzed, numb, unable to move forward, body heavy as stone.

Biologically, it shows up as:

- High cortisol flooding your system.
- Tense muscles that never fully let go.
- A tight chest, shallow breath, or even panic attacks.
- Elevated heart rate and blood pressure.
- Interrupted sleep that leaves you groggy and foggy.
- Lower immunity—your body too taxed to fight infection.
- Inflammation simmering beneath the surface, laying the groundwork for disease.

This is what it means to live under pressure. This is the body in bondage.

We wonder why we're sick. Why fatigue clings to us. Why anxiety feels like the baseline.

Why pain shows up in our joints, our digestion, our hearts. Bondage doesn't just affect our circumstances—it reshapes our cells.

God didn't design us for this.

Freedom isn't just about life being more enjoyable. **Freedom is a healer.** It calms the stress response. It restores rhythm to the nervous system. It strengthens immunity. It teaches the body that it is safe again.

Where bondage breaks down, freedom rebuilds. Where stress steals, freedom restores.

Freedom and Mental Well-being

Freedom is not just a lofty idea—it shows up tangibly in our mental and emotional health. When we feel free, everything inside shifts:

- **Mood lifts.** The heaviness of dread gives way to lightness. You laugh more easily.
- **Energy rises.** No longer drained by constant fear or pressure, your body finds vitality again.
- **Emotional resilience grows.** Challenges still come, but they don't crush you. You bend without breaking.
- **Hopefulness expands.** You can see a tomorrow worth moving toward.
- **Self-worth strengthens.** Freedom reminds you that you are not a cog in a machine—you are a beloved child of God, created with purpose.

When we believe we have the power to choose—our path, our pace, our posture—we experience less anxiety, less depression, and more joy.

Autonomy is not rebellion. It is healing. It is dignity. It is the recognition that your body, mind, and spirit were created to walk in partnership with God, not slavery to fear or expectation.

God did not give us freedom so we could run away from Him. Freedom isn't a ticket to isolation. It isn't throwing off relationship. Freedom is the gift of walking with Him without chains. It's not coerced love—it's chosen love.

Think of the Garden. God could have programmed Adam and Eve to obey, but instead He gave them choice. Why? Because real love requires freedom. And that same freedom He gave then—He gives to you now.

When you live in freedom:

- You stop bracing against God as if He were angry or unsafe.
- You stop hiding in shame, imagining He's waiting to scold you.
- You begin to lean into Him, not out of fear, but because you actually want to.

Freedom transforms your mental well-being because it transforms your relationship with God. Instead of a taskmaster, you find a Father. Instead of pressure, you find presence. Instead of judgment, you find joy.

This is the kind of freedom that makes your nervous system exhale, your thoughts quiet, and your spirit expand. It's not about running away—it's about finally realizing you're safe enough to stay.

Debt, Provision, and Financial Peace

Let's talk about one of the biggest sources of stress in modern life: **money.**

Financial bondage isn't only about bills piling up. It's about the deeper reality of feeling unsafe. Of bracing every time the phone rings because it might be a collector. Of waking up with tight shoulders because you're carrying the weight of debt. Of lying in bed at night rehearsing numbers in your head, trying to figure out if there's enough.

This stress doesn't just live in your mind—it **lives in your body.**

- Cortisol surges and stays high.
- Sleep becomes shallow and broken.
- Digestion slows or goes haywire.
- Muscles lock in chronic tension.
- The immune system weakens, leaving you vulnerable to sickness.

Financial bondage trains the body to exist in **fight-or-flight**, as if every day is survival mode.

Over time, this constant pressure accelerates aging, increases inflammation, and even rewires the brain to expect scarcity as normal.

Here's the truth: **lack is not God's design.**

What if we began to see provision differently—not as something we must claw, hustle, or manipulate to receive, but as a steady flow from the hand of a generous Father? What if we truly believed Him when He says He provides every good and perfect gift?

As we explored in Chapter 6, money is not the root of all evil. It is a neutral tool, a butterfly in the garden, meant to bring beauty, movement, and freedom.

It's the obsession and idolatry of money that destroys. When money is stewarded in love and trust, it becomes a blessing, not a burden.

Financial freedom isn't about luxury. It's about peace.

- Peace that you don't have to sacrifice your health on the altar of hustle.
- Peace that your bills don't determine your worth.
- Peace that you don't have to live in comparison, but in contentment.

And peace heals.

When your body believes it is secure—when you know you are provided for—something shifts inside. The nervous system unwinds. The immune system strengthens. Hormones rebalance. Breath deepens. Your body moves out of survival and into rest, repair, and even creativity.

Freedom—even financial freedom—is healing. It's not about amount or counting. It's about knowing you are rooted in the abundance of God's love, and therefore free to live, give, and rest without fear.

Shame, and Internal Bondage

Bondage isn't just about external systems. It can live quietly—sometimes loudly—in your own beliefs.

Shame is sneaky. It doesn't always shout; often it whispers:

- *"I'm not enough."*
- *"I have to earn love."*
- *"If I let go, everything will fall apart."*

These are not harmless thoughts. They are **chains** that bind the heart and body.

Shame doesn't just stay in your mind—it moves into your body. It feels like:

- A knot in your stomach before you speak.
- Tightness in your chest when you try to rest.
- The shallow breath of someone bracing for rejection.
- The slumped shoulders of someone carrying invisible weight.

It drives us to overwork, over-exercise, over-please. Or to withdraw, numb out, and disconnect. Either way, it cages us inside a life that feels small, unsafe, and unworthy of joy.

Here's the miracle: **Jesus came to set captives free—especially those captive inside.**

He doesn't just open prison doors out in the world—He unlocks the ones in your mind. He speaks into the shame-voice that says, *"You're not enough,"* and answers, *"You are my Beloved."*

When shame loosens its grip, the body feels it too:

- Shoulders lift.
- Breath deepens.
- Muscles soften.
- Joy rises where tension once lived.

When we begin to live unbound, we don't just change our own story— we change the world. A free person carries a presence that liberates others. Your freedom plants seeds of freedom in your family, your community, even your culture.

You were never meant to live braced against life. You were meant to dance with it—open, unashamed, and fully alive in the love of God.

The Garden of Choice

From the very beginning, humanity stood in a garden filled with choices.

The first choice—to eat from the tree of knowledge—led to the *perception* of separation from God.

Even in that moment, God came looking: *"Where are you?"*

God didn't revoke the gift of choice. He didn't install Himself as a dictator. Instead, He continued to honor humanity's freedom, knowing that love without freedom is not love at all.

He still does.

Right now, you stand in your own garden of choices. Each one matters—not because God will love you more or less, but because each choice shapes how your body, spirit, and life align with Him.

- Will I trust—or will I carry it all myself?
- Will I forgive—or let bitterness weigh me down?

- Will I rest—or grind until I collapse?
- Will I be present—or live distracted and disconnected?
- Will I say yes to joy—or rehearse fear and scarcity?

Every choice plants something in your garden. Science even shows that choices affect our biology—lowering or raising stress, balancing or disrupting hormones, strengthening or weakening immunity. **Your body responds to the freedom God has given you.**

Think about that: the Creator of the universe, who knows all things and holds all power, chooses to entrust you with freedom every moment.

He honors your ability to say yes or no, because He values your dignity and loves you without condition.

That realization itself is freeing. You don't have to fear making the wrong move as though God will abandon you.

You get to live in the security of knowing His love is constant, while your freedom remains intact.

The garden of choice is not a test. It's an invitation. Every day, in every decision, you are invited into deeper trust, deeper joy, and deeper embodied freedom.

Fully Present with God

Freedom is not just the absence of chains—it's the presence of peace. These prompts invite you to notice where your spirit longs for release and where your body already knows freedom.

Where in your life do you feel free?

Maybe it's when you walk outside, when you sing, when you pray, when you're with people who love you as you are. Write these places of freedom and give thanks for them.

Where do you feel constrained or powerless?

Be honest. Is it in your work, your health, your finances, or your relationships? Notice how your body feels even as you name these places.

What has your body been holding that you're ready to release?

Stress in your shoulders, tightness in your chest, pressure in your stomach. Write it down. Then, pray a simple prayer: *Father, I place this burden in Your hands.*

What does freedom look like to you—emotionally, financially, spiritually, physically?

Write your vision of freedom. Don't hold back. God delights in your desire for wholeness.

Freedom and Movement

Your body was made to move. Dance, stretch, walk, play—these are acts of freedom. And when you move freely, you stimulate:

- Lymphatic drainage
- Joint lubrication
- Muscle recovery
- Brain balance (bilateral integration)

Movement isn't just exercise. It's embodied liberation.

So dance freely with your Father in joy in this moment and see what your body does!

Spiritual Freedom and Embodied Trust

Freedom in the Spirit doesn't just live in some lofty, unseen realm. It ripples through your very cells. When you begin to trust God deeply—when His love becomes more than an idea and starts to feel like the ground beneath your feet—your body knows.

- Your nervous system resets. The constant bracing eases. The fight-or-flight response steps back.
- Your muscles exhale. The tension you've carried as if the weight of the world rested on your shoulders begins to melt.
- Your pain receptors quiet. Your body no longer screams for attention because it has entered into safety.

This is the power of embodied trust.

The more we yield to divine love, the more our body learns what it feels like to live safe—even in a world that often feels unsafe. Not because there's no danger, but because there is always a Shepherd.

We walk through valleys differently when we walk in freedom. Fear no longer dictates our steps. Anxiety no longer controls our breathing. Scarcity no longer locks us in survival mode.

Spiritual freedom is not escape—it is presence. It is the felt reality that no chain is stronger than His love. That no system, no circumstance, no inner critic can take away the truth: *You are free because He has made you free.*

When that truth lives in your spirit, your body joins the chorus. Cells respond. Hormones regulate. Breath flows. Joy rises. Freedom becomes not just a belief, but a physiology.

This is the miracle of divine love: **the Spirit sets you free, and your body learns how to live as if it's true.**

Closing Blessing

May your breath return to you.
May your muscles soften.
May your nervous system feel safe.
May you know that you are not forced—you are invited.
You are free to walk with God.
You are free to rest.
You are free to create.
You are free to feel joy.
Your freedom is holy.
Your choice is honored.
Your garden is yours to tend.
And you are not alone.

Amen.

Chapter 5

THE PHYSIOLOGY OF CONNECTION WITH GOD AND OTHERS

We were never meant to walk alone. In the very beginning, God walked with Adam and Eve in the cool of the day.

Not as a distant deity, but as a companion. As a presence. As connection.

Love needs relationship. Truth thrives in togetherness. Healing lives in connection.

Our bodies were made to connect. To feel. To trust. To give and receive.

Somewhere along the way, many of us learned to guard instead of open.

To withdraw instead of lean in.

This chapter is a return.

A gentle reminder that connection—with God, with ourselves, and with others—is not just good theology. It's good physiology.

Connection with God

What happens when we feel close to God?

- Cortisol drops
- Peace hormones rise
- Brain shifts to calm, open states
- Our immune response improves

Spiritual practices like prayer, worship, and meditation are more than sacred rituals.

They are nervous system reset buttons.

You don't have to perform for God's attention.

He is already with you. And when your body receives that truth, it begins to heal.

Vulnerability: The Doorway to Connection

True connection requires vulnerability.

- **With the Lord:** To show up honestly, even in your doubt just as you are, all of you.
- **With yourself:** To acknowledge your needs, limits, and longings.
- **With others:** To let someone see the real you—messy, miraculous, and in process.

Vulnerability isn't weakness.

It's courage. It opens the body. It opens the spirit. It opens the garden.

Trust: The Soil of Safe Connection

Trust is the fertile ground in which all true connection grows. Without it, relationships—whether with God, with others, or even within ourselves—wither. With it, they flourish.

- **Trusting the Lord** means believing that His intentions toward you are always good, even when life feels uncertain. It is resting in His character, His promises, and His presence. This kind of trust lifts the burden of self-reliance and allows your body to release its constant vigilance.
- **Trusting yourself** is just as vital. It's choosing to believe that the Spirit of God lives within you, guiding your instincts, your creativity, and your body's wisdom. When you trust yourself, you stop fighting your own signals and start honoring them—whether it's hunger, fatigue, intuition, or desire.
- **Trusting others** does not mean naïveté or blind vulnerability. It means allowing safe people into your life and giving your heart permission to receive love. Trusting others is a risk, but it is also the doorway to intimacy, belonging, and joy.

When trust is present, the body knows. It relaxes. Muscles soften. Breath deepens. The heartbeat steadies. The nervous system shifts out of defense and into connection.

In trust, you are no longer bracing against life. You are receiving it. You are no longer hiding behind armor. You are letting yourself be seen, known, and loved.

Trust is not just a choice of the mind—it is the soil of the body, where connection takes root and grows strong.

When that soil is tended, your relationships—with God, with yourself, and with others—become gardens where love can truly flourish.

Connection and the Body: A Love Story

Connection isn't just an emotional experience—it's a whole-body love story. When you are truly connected—to God, to yourself, to others—your body knows it.

Here's what happens physiologically when we are living in connection:

- **Anxiety decreases, peace increases.** The nervous system shifts from fight-or-flight into rest-and-digest. Shoulders drop. Breath deepens.
- **Heart health strengthens.** Blood pressure stabilizes. Rhythms even out. Stress hormones calm.
- **Resilience grows.** Your body bounces back from challenges more easily.
- **Immunity rises.** The body literally heals faster when it feels safe and connected.
- **Depression decreases, joy rises.** Connection fills the body with neurotransmitters like serotonin and oxytocin, which elevate mood and increase hope.

Connection is not a luxury. It is holy medicine, woven into our very design.

Connection with Ourselves

You cannot deeply connect with others—or even with God—if you are at war within yourself. Connection begins here.

What does connection to self feel like?

- Breath that moves easily to your belly instead of stopping in your chest.
- Permission to rest without guilt, knowing your worth isn't tied to productivity.
- Welcoming your emotions as messengers, not enemies.
- Compassion for your limitations, seeing them as part of your humanity, not evidence of failure.

This is self-stewardship. When you care for yourself, you are aligning with how God designed you to flourish.

When we connect with ourselves, our bodies shift:

- The heart beats steadier and with more ease.
- Sleep becomes deeper and more restorative.
- Pain levels decrease, because the body is no longer bracing against itself.

To connect with yourself is to say: *I choose to live with myself, not against myself.*

Connection with Others

From the very beginning of life, we are wired for connection. Infants placed on their mother's chest calm almost instantly. The same wiring continues into adulthood.

The body's response to connection is profound:

- Skin-to-skin contact stabilizes not only newborns but adults too, reducing stress and lowering blood pressure.
- A warm hug or gentle touch decreases pain and increases serotonin, boosting mood and creating safety.
- Eye contact tells the nervous system, *you are seen, you belong.*
- Shared laughter floods the body with healing hormones, strengthening immunity and deepening bonds.

True connection looks like:

- Listening to understand, not just to reply.
- Allowing yourself to be seen and known, without masks or performance.
- Staying curious about others' experiences, instead of rushing to judgment.
- Showing up as you are—imperfect, real, and present.

When we connect with others in love, our bodies become instruments of healing—for ourselves and for those we touch.

Barriers to Connection

Sometimes we long for connection and yet find ourselves pulling away from it. Why? Because somewhere along the way, connection became unsafe.

Barriers often look like:

- **Fear of rejection.** The thought, *If I open up, I'll be left or judged.* The body tightens, the chest braces, the breath shortens.
- **Past trauma.** Old wounds whisper that closeness equals danger. Muscles tense, eyes avert, the nervous system stays on guard.
- **Busyness.** We fill our calendars so full that there's no space to be truly present. The pace numbs the ache of loneliness but never satisfies it.
- **Shame.** That quiet, heavy voice that says, *If they knew the real me, they'd turn away.* Shame curls us inward, pulling us away from love.

These barriers are not signs of weakness or failure—they are signs of injury. Like a physical wound, they form protective scar tissue. Scar tissue can soften, stretch, and heal.

The good news? Connection never comes as a demand. It is always an invitation. Gentle. Patient. Loving.

God Himself models this—He knocks, but He never forces His way in. And we can navigate these barriers with the same grace, choosing small, steady steps toward trust again.

From Isolation to Integration

Our culture often praises independence as strength: *I can do this on my own. I don't need anyone.* But the body tells a different story. The body was designed for interdependence.

Just look within:

- **Cells** communicate constantly, sending signals of repair, growth, and need.
- **Organs** support one another in balance—your heart cannot pump without oxygen from your lungs, your brain cannot think without fuel from your digestive system.
- **The nervous system** calms when it hears a safe tone of voice, when it feels the warmth of touch, when it senses another presence nearby.

Even in our biology, isolation creates imbalance. Integration creates life.

Spiritually, too, this is our design. The Trinity is a relationship—a divine dance of love between Father, Son, and Spirit. And we were created in that image: made for communion, not separation.

When we live isolated, the body feels it: fatigue deepens, stress rises, depression lingers.

When we live integrated—with God, with ourselves, with others—the body responds: energy rises, immunity strengthens, joy multiplies.

Isolation says, *I must hold it all alone.*

Integration whispers, *We're in this together.*

Fully Present with God

We are not made to grow alone. These prompts help you notice where connection is alive in your life and where God may be inviting you to open more.

- **Where in your life are you practicing vulnerability?**
  Vulnerability is the soil where intimacy grows. Write down where you've dared to be open—even in small ways.
- **Do you feel safe to trust—God, yourself, others?**
  Reflect on where trust comes easily, and where fear still whispers. How does your body feel when you lean into trust?
- **What relationships bring you life?**
  Think of the people who refresh you. How do you feel in their presence—lighter, calmer, more yourself? Write about the fruits of these connections.
- **What kind of connection are you longing for more of?**
  Deeper intimacy with God? More joy with friends? A more open relationship with your spouse? Name your longing before the Father who calls you beloved.

_____

_____

_____

_____

_____

_____

_____

_____

_____

_____

_____

Spiritual Connection and the Nervous System

Spiritual connection is not just a lofty idea—it is embodied. When we connect with God, it is not only our soul that feels the difference. Our body responds. Our nervous system shifts into safety. Our biology remembers its original design.

Connection with God:

- **Reduces anxiety and depression.** Fear quiets because Love is present.
- **Increases resilience.** Stress doesn't disappear, but the body recovers faster because it no longer feels alone.
- **Brings order to scattered minds.** Thoughts that spiral in chaos are gathered and calmed by His voice.

Physiologically, this feels like:

- **Restorative sleep.** The kind that leaves you renewed, not just rested.
- **Deep breathing.** Lungs filling fully, exhaling completely, oxygen flowing freely.
- **Gentle movement.** Muscles softening, joints opening, the body moving in harmony instead of bracing in resistance.

When you walk with God, your body experiences Eden again. Safety. Abundance. Belonging. Your nervous system learns what it was made for: not survival mode, but communion.

This is why Jesus said, *"Abide in Me."* Abiding isn't abstract—it's embodied. It's the exhale of knowing you are held. It's your heart rate slowing as trust replaces fear. It's your body releasing tension because your spirit remembers: *I am not alone. I am deeply loved.*

The more we live connected to Him, the more heaven's rhythm becomes our rhythm—slow, steady, peaceful, joyful. And that rhythm heals.

You were made to walk with God, not as a distant deity but as your very Source. And when you do, every cell, every breath, every heartbeat remembers Eden—and leans toward eternity.

Closing Blessing

May you be gently known.
May you be lovingly held.
May you feel safe enough to soften.
May you trust God's voice in the silence.
May you trust your own heart.
May you trust that others can hold space for you, too.

You were made to be connected. Not just spiritually. Not just emotionally. But biologically.

Your body was designed for love. And you are never, ever alone.

Amen.

Chapter 6

THE PHYSIOLOGY OF FAITH

W hat does it mean to trust what you cannot see? To lean your full weight on something invisible—and discover it holds?

Faith is not superstition or wishful thinking. It is a steadying presence, a precious inner compass. Faith lives in the body as much as it does in the spirit. It anchors you when reason runs out.

It whispers: *I may not know the way, but I know the One who walks with me.*

Trust is not passive—it is a bold act of vulnerability. It is surrender to Love in the face of uncertainty. And that surrender does something profound to our bodies.

This thread of trust has woven itself through my life and work before—most profoundly in *The River*, my first book and testimony. That story was about learning to trust in the middle of death and resurrection:

- Trusting God when everything looked lost.
- Trusting others in raw vulnerability after trauma.
- Trusting myself again after seasons of confusion and doubt.

Every moment of healing in that story began not with control, but with trust.

That same invitation flows into this garden. Faith is not knowing every detail of the ending.

It is choosing to walk with the One who does.

Faith isn't something you muster up by force. It's a posture of resting in the One who is already holding you. And when your spirit leans into that truth, your body begins to follow—into peace, into clarity, into life.

Your Faith Has Healed You

These words echo again and again in Scripture: *"Your faith has healed you."*

Notice what Jesus does **not** say. He doesn't say, *"I healed you by My power alone."* He doesn't say, *"The rules healed you."*

He looks into the eyes of men and women who dared to trust Him, and He names the truth already at work within them: *"Your faith has healed you."*

This is revolutionary. It shifts healing from something we wait passively to receive into something we participate in—an embodied collaboration with God.

Faith is not magic. Faith is alignment. It is the act of saying yes to what God has already placed within us—the power to restore, renew, and regenerate.

What kind of power lives in trust?

When we believe in God's goodness, the body itself begins to change:

- Muscles soften where tension once ruled.
- The heart opens, blood flow improves, circulation expands.
- The mind calms, releasing new neural pathways of possibility.
- The nervous system shifts from defense into rest and repair.

Faith isn't just invisible—it is physiological. It opens the floodgates of healing.

This is where the mystery of faith meets what many today call *manifestation*. Jesus never used that word, but He embodied its truth: "As you believe, so it will be."

Faith is creative. It speaks life where there was death. It imagines wholeness where the world has only declared brokenness. It manifests new realities because it aligns our inner being—spirit, soul, and body—with the truth of God's kingdom.

The woman who touched the hem of Jesus' robe believed healing was possible—and her body responded. The blind man who cried out believed sight was available—and his eyes opened.

Again and again, Jesus pointed not just to His divinity, but to the miracle already alive in human trust.

Faith is not about denying pain or pretending weakness doesn't exist.

It is about **choosing to align with God's infinite goodness rather than the world's limited scripts.**

It is about stepping into the reality that our bodies were designed to heal, to adapt, to flourish—because that is the imprint of heaven.

Your faith can create your reality. Not because you are manufacturing something out of thin air, but because you are agreeing with what God already said is true: *"I have come that they may have life, and have it abundantly."*

Healing, joy, peace, freedom—these are not far-off promises. They are the fruit of trust, here and now. When you believe, your cells remember Eden. When you trust, your body begins to align with heaven's design.

Your faith has healed you. These are not just words for someone else in Scripture. They are words for you. Today.

Why Do We Doubt?

Because we're human.
Because life can be hard.
Because what we see often contradicts what we hope.

The brain, designed for survival, clings to what it knows.

Doubt can be a defense mechanism—a way to brace, to protect, to manage disappointment.

What if we gently invited the brain to trust again? Not with shame. Not with pressure. But with love.

Jesus met doubters with kindness. He showed his wounds. He fed them breakfast. He walked with them.

Your doubt is not a threat to God. And it doesn't cancel your faith. It can become the doorway back into belief.

Faith in the Body: What Happens When We Believe

Faith is not just an idea—it's an embodied reality. When we believe, our biology shifts to match what our spirit has embraced.

Here's what science and Scripture both affirm happens when faith takes root:

- **Faith re-patterns the mind.** Belief literally rewires the brain, creating new neural pathways of peace, safety, and possibility.
- **Faith lowers stress chemistry.** Cortisol levels decrease, reducing inflammation and protecting the body against chronic illness.
- **Faith strengthens immunity.** The body responds to hope and trust by mobilizing defenses and increasing resilience.
- **Faith extends vitality.** Faith-practicing individuals often live longer, healthier lives—not because they are spared struggle, but because their bodies are continually renewed in the atmosphere of trust.
- **Faith anchors us in hope.** It roots us in a bigger story than our pain or fear, keeping us steady when the storm rages.

Faith is not superstition. It is physiology. It is heaven incarnating into the cells of our bodies.

Trusting God, Ourselves, and Others

Faith always shows up as trust. *Trust, trust, trust.* It was the heartbeat of *The River,* and it is the heartbeat of this garden too.

Trust is what allows faith to move from the unseen to the tangible. It is what bridges the gap between promise and experience. Without trust, faith stays abstract. With trust, faith becomes flesh.

Trust is not naive. It doesn't mean ignoring danger or pretending everything is fine. Trust is active alignment—it says:

- **I trust God.** Not because I understand everything, but because He has called me Beloved, and His character is love.
- **I trust myself.** Not because I am flawless, but because God has placed His Spirit in me, and my body is a temple worthy of kindness.
- **I trust others.** Not blindly, but with discernment—opening to the possibility of companionship, healing, and growth in community.

When trust lives in the body, here's what it feels like:

- Muscles unclench.
- Breath deepens.
- The heart steadies.
- The nervous system shifts from bracing to belonging.

Trust doesn't erase uncertainty. It carries us through it. It says: *Even when I don't see the whole picture, I will keep walking.*

And as we walk—in faith, in trust—our bodies learn a new rhythm. The rhythm of Eden. The rhythm of freedom. The rhythm of Love.

Great Faith: Whose Eyes?

What is "great faith"?

To the world, it often looks like certainty. Strength. Unshakeable conviction.

In the eyes of God?

Great faith might look like a trembling hand reaching out.

Or a whisper: "Help my unbelief."

Or simply showing up, one breath at a time.

Or turning around—believing the healing of a loved one is as good as done.

God doesn't measure faith by human standards. He measures it by trust.

Fully Present with God

Faith is not just an idea—it lives in the body, steadying breath and softening fear. These prompts invite you to notice where faith is alive in you and where it longs to deepen.

- **Where is your faith anchored today?**
  Is it in God's goodness? In your own efforts? In what others say? Write where your trust truly rests.
- **What has shaped your trust in God, yourself, or others?**
  Think back on your story—times of answered prayer, times of disappointment, times of unexpected provision. How has each one shaped your heart?
- **What would it feel like to surrender a little more?**
  Notice your body as you consider surrender. Does your jaw unclench? Does your breathing slow? Write how surrender shows up physically for you.
- **Can you name a time your faith shifted something in your body?**
  Maybe peace washed away anxiety, or trust gave you courage to act. Write this memory as a testimony of God's faithfulness.

_____

_____

_____

_____

_____

_____

_____

_____

_____

_____

Faith and Vision

Faith is not only trust—it is sight. It opens the eyes of the heart to see beyond the visible. To glimpse what is possible before it takes form. To live as if what God has promised is already here.

This kind of vision reshapes both spirit and body:

- **Vision beyond the visible fosters motivation.** When we see hope, the body generates energy to move toward it.
- **Anticipation of good strengthens immunity.** The expectation of life, joy, and abundance literally enhances the body's defenses.
- **Imagining possibility engages creative neural networks.** The same parts of the brain that design art, music, and innovation ignite when we imagine what God can do.

This is holy imagination—your God-given capacity to see with Heaven's eyes.

It is not wishful thinking.
It is not denial.
It is participation in divine creativity.

Faith is your holy imagination partnered with Heaven. It is vision aligning with Love to co-create a new reality.

Eyes Opened to the Infinite

In 2 Kings 6:17, the prophet Elisha prayed, *"Open his eyes, Lord, so that he may see."* And suddenly the servant's eyes were opened—not to earthly scarcity, but to the hills full of heavenly horses and chariots of fire.

That is the invitation of faith: to have our vision expanded. To look beyond fear and impossibility and glimpse the infinite resources of Heaven surrounding us.

When faith opens our eyes, we:

- See angels encamped where others see enemies.

- See provision where others see lack.
- See health where others see decline.
- See future where others see endings.

Faith as Creative Sight

Imagination is not childish. It is divine.

It is the faculty through which God paints His promises on the canvas of your inner world.

Every breakthrough begins with someone imagining differently:

- Abraham pictured descendants as numerous as the stars.
- Moses envisioned a people walking free.
- Mary envisioned the impossible—the Word made flesh within her womb.

Faith asks us to see like this: not confined by what has been, but wide open to what God says is possible.

When you dare to imagine with God, your body participates:

- Dopamine rises with hope.
- Neural pathways fire in alignment with possibility.
- Your physiology prepares to step into what your spirit has already seen.

Faith and vision are not about escaping reality.

They are about transforming it.

They are Heaven's eyes opening in your body, guiding you to walk in creativity, freedom, and infinite possibility.

Closing Blessing

May your faith feel like breath—present, gentle, sustaining.
May your body relax by knowing that you are held.
May trust take root in your cells.
May your nervous system feel safe in God's timing.

You are not alone in your questions.
Your faith is not measured by perfection.
God sees the spark. He calls it great.

Amen.

Chapter 7

THE PHYSIOLOGY OF KINDNESS

Kindness is the heart of Heaven on display.
It is not weakness. It is not performance.

It is the strength to move toward another in love—without agenda, without pretense, without needing anything in return.

Niceness is often about appearances. It's people-pleasing, conflict-avoiding, smiling when we want to cry.

Kindness is different. It's rooted in truth and freedom. It is Heaven flowing through us—meeting needs, offering presence, telling the truth in love.

Scripture says it clearly: *It is God's kindness that leads us to repentance.* Not fear. Not shame. Not threats. Kindness.

And when we live in that flow—giving and receiving kindness—our bodies, our relationships, and our communities thrive.

Giving and Receiving Kindness

For many of us, one side of kindness feels easier than the other.

- Maybe you pour yourself out for others, but when kindness comes back to you, you deflect it: *"Oh, you didn't have to..."*

- Maybe you love receiving kindness, but struggle to extend it—worried it will cost too much or be misunderstood.
- Maybe you were taught that kindness has to be earned—or that it's weakness, a soft trait in a hard world.

God's kindness is never transactional. It is free.

Freely you have received—freely give.

When we give and receive kindness without condition, it doesn't just shape our spirits. It rewires our biology.

The Physiology of Kindness

Kindness is not sentimental—it is *somatic*. It takes root in the body. Here's what science and scripture agree on:

- **Nervous System Regulation**: Acts of kindness calm the fight-or-flight response and activate "rest-and-digest." Muscles relax. Heart rate slows. Breath deepens.
- **Reduced Inflammation**: Kindness literally lowers markers of inflammation, protecting against disease.
- **Cardiovascular Health**: It protects the heart, reduces blood pressure, and increases resilience against stress.
- **Immunity & Recovery**: People who practice kindness heal faster, fight infections more effectively, and even recover quicker from surgeries or illness.
- **Mental Health**: Kindness decreases anxiety and depression, while increasing joy, contentment, and satisfaction with life.
- **Longevity**: Communities marked by kindness consistently live longer, healthier lives.
- **Contagion Effect**: One act of kindness inspires another, rippling across bodies, families, and entire communities.

Kindness is not just spiritual virtue—it is embodied medicine.

Kindness and Muscle, Metabolism, and Energy

Kindness doesn't just touch the mind or emotions—it changes the way your body *functions*:

- **Muscle Health**: When we live in fear or anger, the body tightens. Chronic stress accumulates as knots in the shoulders, clenched jaws, and stiff backs. Kindness releases these tensions, restoring fluid movement and encouraging physical activity rooted in joy, not punishment.
- **Metabolism**: Kindness lowers cortisol, the stress hormone that keeps blood sugar unstable and weight retention high. When we step into kindness, our body shifts from survival mode to rest-and-digest. Digestion improves. Energy stabilizes. Fatigue lessens.
- **Hormonal Balance**: Acts of kindness boost oxytocin, the bonding hormone, which brings warmth, trust, and motivation. This single hormone has ripple effects—supporting reproductive health, thyroid balance, and even slowed aging.

Even the smallest act—a smile, a prayer, a word of encouragement—sets off these cascades in the body.

Kindness and Community

Kindness doesn't stay private. It builds ecosystems.

- In communities marked by kindness, health improves collectively. Hormones balance, immunity rises, and resilience deepens.
- Belonging becomes medicine. Loneliness is one of the greatest predictors of disease and early death—kindness is the antidote.
- Love flows more freely when the soil of kindness is present.

Your body doesn't just thrive on personal kindness—it flourishes when immersed in a culture of kindness.

Kindness vs. Niceness

This is critical: niceness is not the same as kindness.

I struggled with the difference most of my early life. Now, I'm free to be lovingly kind without the trap of "people-pleasing".

- Niceness avoids conflict. Kindness tells the truth with love.
- Niceness seeks approval. Kindness seeks the good of the other.
- Niceness wears a mask. Kindness removes it.
- Niceness can leave the body tight, resentful, and exhausted. Kindness frees the body—because it flows from volition, not obligation.

True kindness doesn't mean always saying yes. Sometimes it means setting a boundary.

Sometimes it means saying, "This isn't healthy for me." That, too, is love.

When we embody kindness—not as performance, but as presence—our bodies rest. Our nervous systems trust. Our spirits open.

Kindness as Heaven's Pulse

In Eden, everything thrived in relationship. And at the center of those relationships was kindness—the rhythm of giving and receiving without fear.

Kindness is the pulse of Heaven. It nourishes every part of the internal garden:

- Kindness to yourself: resting without guilt, forgiving your own humanity, speaking gently to your body.
- Kindness to others: meeting them where they are without agenda, extending the same grace you've received.
- Kindness to God: trusting His voice of love, not suspicion or fear.

When kindness becomes the rhythm of your life, your body carries the signature of Heaven.

Kindness is not small. It is not soft. It is not weakness.

It is strength, safety, freedom, and presence—woven into your very cells.

Kindness heals.

Fully Present with God

Kindness is one of the simplest, most powerful ways the Spirit flows through us. These prompts invite you to notice the rhythm of kindness in your life and body.

- **When do you feel most kind?**
  Is it when you're rested? When you're connected to God? When you're serving someone else? Reflect on what helps kindness naturally rise in you.
- **How do you respond to kindness from others?**
  Do you receive it with ease—or deflect it, feeling unworthy? Write what it feels like in your body to truly receive kindness.
- **Are you kind to your own body, thoughts, and rhythms?**
  Do you let yourself rest? Do you speak gently to yourself? Do you honor your body's signals? Be honest here—kindness begins within.
- **What small act of kindness could you offer today?**
  To your spouse, a friend, a stranger, or even yourself. Write it down and, if you can, act on it today.

_____

_____

_____

_____

_____

_____

_____

_____

_____

_____

_____

Closing Blessing

May kindness be the rhythm of your body.
May your breath deepen and your muscles soften.
May you give without striving. Receive without guilt. And offer your presence like sunlight.

You are not too much.
You are not too little.
You are exactly enough.

And kindness lives in you.

Amen.

Conclusion

RETURN TO THE GARDEN

We've walked together now, you and I.
Through the gates of remembrance.
Through questions of identity, healing, joy, rest, and trust.
Through Eden—not as myth or metaphor, but as your living reality.

And here we are.
Not at the end.
But standing at a threshold.
A new beginning.
A return.
A re-entry into your own body as sacred ground, as temple, as dwelling place where God delights to live.

You are not separate from wellness.
You are not distant from Eden.
You were never disqualified.
Not by pain. Not by trauma. Not by the years that felt wasted or the diagnoses that tried to define you.

You were made in love.
And in the presence of God's love, nothing is ever truly lost. Every broken piece is gathered. Every season is redeemed. Every scar becomes part of the story of restoration.

Maybe you picked up this book looking for a roadmap, a program, a protocol.
Instead, what you've found is relationship.
With your body. With God. With the garden within you.

This has never been about adding more to your to-do list. It's about remembering.
Remembering who you are.
Remembering whose you are.
Remembering that you are the garden. You are the temple. You are the place where Heaven and Earth embrace.

The River taught me to surrender. To trust the current, even when it carried me through death and into resurrection.
This garden has taught me to live.
To receive, to play, to dance with God in the soil of daily life.
To co-create beauty with Him in every breath, every choice, every relationship.

Now I pass the invitation to you:
Keep walking.
Keep listening.
Keep trusting.

Don't force. Don't strive. Don't fix.
Just be.

Let your body speak its truth.
Let God tend the places that ache.
Let your muscles relax into peace.
Let your nervous system learn safety again.
Let your heart grow wide with hope, and your spirit learn what freedom feels like in your bones.

You are allowed to be well.
You are allowed to be whole.
You are allowed to feel joy in your body.
You are allowed to rest, to play, to question, to grow, to enjoy.

This is not indulgence—it is design.
This is not luxury—it is love.
This is what you were created for.

This journey doesn't end here. It begins here—every time you say yes
to divine presence in your daily life.

Every breath, a prayer.
Every choice, a seed.
Every act of care, a tending of what is holy.

Let love be your rhythm.
Let rest be your reset.
Let joy be your compass.
Let trust be your soil.
Let light be your atmosphere.

And so, I bless you:

I bless you to be abundantly well—your body radiant, flowing in the
Father's light that is also your own.
I bless you to receive continuous, miraculous healing—the truest
nature of your being—receiving the infinite good of your Creator,
releasing all that no longer belongs.
I bless you to play, to create, to live in the freedom of the beloved child
you have always been, before the world tried to tell you otherwise.
I bless you to be free.
To be love.
To be light.
Just like your Father—whose image you bear.

Until we meet again—in spirit, on the page, in prayer, or in Heaven's
garden—
May your soil be nourished.
May your garden bloom.
May your steps be guided.
May your health be whole.
May your joy be contagious.

You are not alone.
You never were.

And this—this is only the beginning.

With infinite love,
Nicholas

www.ingramcontent.com/pod-product-compliance
Lightning Source LLC
Chambersburg PA
CBHW051512120626
46551CB00012B/890